INTRODUCTION

Open-mindedness. Being a believer requires open-mindedness. How many people would believe at an early age that there is a man who can heal the sick and raise the dead? That there is a man who was willing to die for people who were yet to be born just so we can have life more abundantly? That there is a man who is *in* you, around you, with you, and above you at all times? That there is a man who fed 5,000 with a meal fit for five...a man who parted seas...a man who walked on water and did not drown...a man—a God? Being a believer begins with open-mindedness.

Annually, my fiancée and I write goals for the year—four for me, four for her, four for us. Then, we pick a word for the year—one for me, one for her, one for us. Our words for this year are favor, wisdom, and excess. The both of us have seen these manifestations in our lives thus far this year. One of my personal goals was to form a secondary avenue of income. When writing the goal, I had no clue what it would look like, where to begin, or even what was in store. Little did I know that on January 2, 2023, while my fiancée Carmen and I read a devotional given to us from a family-friend, that this book would be birthed.

Prior to the new year (2023), I frequently told my fiancée that I never—in almost 25 years of living—felt so joyful and optimistic going into a new year having just lost my life (my mother—God rest her soul) just seven months previously. My mother was a bible reader. She read every word from Genesis to Isaiah—until she had passed away. She would so frequently tell me how fascinating it was to read and how much more intimate of a relationship she felt with Christ because of her studies.

As I too, seek to read every word of the Word, I wrote this book—Through Me: 66 Days of Daily Devotion & Sermonettes for a Life of Godliness—to reach those who do not necessarily have the time or the will or the energy to read the entire bible, but to get a better understanding of its content by applying Scripture to our lives. Reflecting the 66 books in the bible are 66 days (one day from each chapter) that offers an introduction to the topic, a continuation of the biblical narrative, application and next steps. Each page lists the title, foundational Scripture, text, thought questions, and a prayer—all to help guide you on a deeper journey to Godliness.

I ask that as you navigate these next 66 days that you do so with a greater sense of open-mindedness. Receive every word and let God lead the way. Although this is my introduction, I declare and decree that this is your introduction to bigger, your introduction to better, your introduction to higher, your introduction to greater. Whether this is the beginning of your spiritual journey or if you are right in the middle of it, I hope my words speak life into you, giving you the courage, determination, and inspiration to face even the darkest of days.

While this may be designed to introduce myself to you, allow me to introduce the true author of this book: our Lord and Savior, Jesus Christ. I, the pen; he, the words. Here ye him.

DEDICATION

To my mother in heaven, Hazel Lorraine DeLesline

TABLE OF CONTENTS

TABLE OF CONTENTS

GET SOME REST

Genesis 2:1-3

Day 1

Genesis 2: 1-3, *New Living Translation*

- *So the creation of the heavens and the earth and everything in them was completed. On the seventh day God had finished his work of creation, so he rested from all his work. And God blessed the seventh day and declared it holy, because it was the day when he rested from all his work of creation.*

Have you noticed the increasing number of products and services that are supposed to save us time and money: GPS, cellphones, online shopping, paper products...the list goes on and on? Yet, despite these time-saving products, many of us are still burned out, exhausted, tired, and even restless, proving that some of our precious time saving products aren't working. Is it possible that what we lack is not time, but adequate rest? What we need is not a new time saving gadget, but to find the rest that Jesus gives to us.

Genesis, the first book of the bible, introduces us to the major players: God, the Devil, Adam and Eve. In Genesis 2: 1-3, God had finished his first week on the job. On day one he created the heavens and the earth; on day two: the sky; on day three: vegetation; on day four: the sun, moon and stars; on day five: sea creatures and birds; on day six: land animals and man; and finally on day seven: he rested. The text states in Genesis 2:1-3: "So the creation of the heavens and the earth and everything in them was completed. On the seventh day God had finished his work of creation, so he rested from all his work. And God blessed the seventh day and declared it holy, because it was the day when he rested from all his creation" (New Living Translation).

Although I am unaware of when you are reading this, I find myself writing this during the holiday season—though it is rewarding—can also be very exhausting: mentally, emotionally, socially, and even spiritually. We get so busy making meals, entertaining and/or hosting loved ones, shopping, decorating—while still having to manage our daily responsibilities that we perform throughout the week: careers, children, family, finances etc. But God gave us the answer in Genesis 2, for even he, a God of who can see all, be all, hear all, do all, know all, control all and be everywhere at *all* can take a rest after creating his greatest work of creation, why do we feel we are exempt from resting? As another example, in Mark 4: 35, Jesus and his disciples encounter a fierce storm and Scripture writes as the storm came up, "Jesus was sleeping at the back of the boat with his head on a cushion" (Mark 4:35, New Living Translation). Jesus, the one who knows all and sees all, knew this storm was coming, but what did he do? He rested—proactively.

In our lives, we too, face many storms: storms of anxiety, depression, restlessness, health complications, financial hardship, pain, grief and many others, but we cannot allow these inevitable storms of life to deter us from receiving adequate, proactive rest. A recent study of more than 18,000 people in 134 different countries found that 68% of people feel they do not get enough rest. Further, participants stated they typically rest when they are sick, when they have concluded with the activities of the day or week, or when they have just completed a strenuous task. Notice that in each of these cases, rest is the effect of something and not the cause. We often use rest reactively after we`ve worked and worn ourselves out. I want to challenge you today to make your rest proactive.

The bible teaches in 1st Peter 4:12, "Dear friends, don't be surprised at the fiery trials you are going through, as if something strange were happening to you" (New Living Translation). These trials of life are simply things we live through being members of the body of Christ; so if that is the case, why can't we choose to rest proactively so that when these trials, troubles, and tests do arise, we are ready to face them in full strength—spiritually, mentally, emotionally, and even physically. Rome was not conquered in one day, nor was the world created in one. Take time to rest.

Questions:

1. What does rest mean or look like to you?
2. When do you rest?
3. Do you tend to rest proactively or reactively? Why?
4. How can you carve out time to rest?

Prayer:

Father, I thank you for your rest. Help me to rest proactively to reset and regulate my mind, body, and soul. I ask that as I rest physically, that you allow me to rest in your word, your will, and your way. In Jesus` name I pray. Amen.

OUT OF SIGHT, OUT OF MIND

Exodus 14:13

Day 2

Exodus 14:13, *New King James Version*

- *And Moses said to the people, "Do not be afraid. Stand still, and see the salvation of the Lord, which He will accomplish for you today. For the Egyptians whom you see today, you shall see again no more forever.*

Having a career as an educator, we are taught extensively of educational psychology. One of these psychologists, Jean Piaget, developed four stages of cognitive development, describing how children age cognitively from age 0 to about age 12. The first stage of development according to Piaget is Sensorimotor, in which children begin to coordinate senses, become curious about the world, and achieve object permanence or the mentality that although one cannot physically see an object, that the object still exists. In other words, "out of sight, out of mind."

In this Scripture, God is teaching Moses and the Israelites of object **im**permanence. As Moses and the Israelites fled from slavery and oppression under the Lord's direction, the Lord commanded Moses to take a detour so that King Pharaoh would believe the Israelites were lost. God had a plan in place to display his power and Moses obeyed. Pharaoh redacted his decision to free the Israelites and decided to chase after them. As Pharaoh and his army approached, the Israelites became disheartened, leading Moses to declare, "Do not be afraid. Stand still, and see the salvation of the Lord, which He will accomplish for you today. For the Egyptians whom you see today, you shall see again no more forever" (Exodus 14:13, New Living Translation). With the Red Sea in front of them, the Egyptians behind them, and mountains to their left and their right, the Israelites became frantic and fearful. The bible uses the word "camp", stating the Egyptians were camped by the Red Sea. A camp is a temporary accommodation, not a permanent residence; therefore, the Egyptians were not tied to this place, but given passage to go forward. God commanded Moses to raise his staff, to which the Lord parted the Red Sea so the Israelites could escape; as the Egyptians traversed the sea, God commanded Moses to raise his staff a second time, engulfing the Egyptians in water, sweeping them into the sea. Not a single Egyptian survived.

The lesson in this story is two-fold: whatever you may have done in your past is behind you. Don't keep dwelling on what hurt you in the past. Those trials and tribulations are behind you; out of sight, out of mind. Secondly, remember that just because we cannot physically see the Lord, does not mean he is not with us. The Israelites were frantic seeing the presence of the Egyptians, but Moses told them you may see the enemy today, but you will see them no more. Although your campsite may appear fearful, go forward to your destiny! Out of sight, out of mind. Look ahead to the Lord and not back to your previous pains, mistakes, issues, or sins. Out of sight, out of mind; leave the past behind. Move forward!

Questions:

1. What pain, mistakes, issues, or sins have you committed in the past that still haunt you today?
2. What can you do to overcome your past so that you can propel to your future?
3. What can you do daily to remember that although you cannot see the Lord, that he is still with you?
4. How can you continually exhibit an "out of sight, out of mind" mentality when it comes to challenges of your past?

Prayer:

Father, you tell me in your Word that you will never leave me nor forsake me—allow me to never forget that. I pray you help me leave my past behind, for it is out of my sight and therefore out of my mind. Help me to reflect on my past, but do not allow my past to haunt and hinder the blessings and the calling of my prosperous future. I declare victory! In Jesus` name I pray. Amen.

DON`T MAKE GOD SICK

Leviticus 18:24-25

Day 3

Leviticus 18: 24-25, *Contemporary English Version*

- *Don't make yourselves unclean by any of these disgusting practices of those nations that I am forcing out of the land for you. They made themselves and the land so unclean, that I punished the land because of their sins, and I made it vomit them up.*

Vomiting is often a result of the body ridding itself of harmful substances from the stomach or gut. Oftentimes we hear commercials for specific medications that include vomiting as a side effect of taking the medication. Furthermore, COVID, the flu, stomach viruses and even bacteria such as E. coli and salmonella may result in vomiting—again ridding the body of harmful substances. In Scripture, that harmful substance is sin.

The book of Leviticus is a book of laws and rituals intended for the Levites, or the priests of the Israelites. The book of Leviticus informs the Levites of types of offerings, priestly ordinations, clean and unclean animals and practices, skin diseases, sexual practices, festivals, and consequences of disobedience. In the 18th chapter, the Lord is teaching Moses of forbidden sexual practices of the people in Egypt (where the Israelites used to live) and Canaan (where God is leading them). In modern times, we might consider these forbidden practices incestual. After giving instruction, God declares to Moses to be mindful of such practices that could deem the Israelites unclean, warning them to not engage in these forbidden practices as God caused the land to vomit out these nations. God continues, "If any of you do these vulgar disgusting things, you will be unclean and no longer belong to my people. I am the Lord your God..." (Leviticus 18: 30, Contemporary English Version).

To be more transparent, it is the sins of these nations that caused the Lord to vomit them out. Don`t be like these nations by forcing God to vomit you out of his will or his way by succumbing to not only sexual sin, but any type of sin. Just because your friends, your family, your co-workers, or even your fellow church-folks do it, does not mean it is of God. The world often pressures people into sin because the world deems the sin "alright" as it has become so common (sex before marriage, homosexuality, gambling, drunkenness—just to name a few), but remember that despite these many sins, one thing remains constant: our Father. Don't become so engulfed in the sins of the world that God sees fit to vomit you out of his will. God does offer us all a remedy to rid or "vomit" the sickness of sin within us: "If we confess our sins, he is faithful and just to forgive us our sins and to cleanse us from all unrighteousness" (1 John 1:9, English Standard Version). Don't make God sick, but rather be a symptom of his health by confessing your sins and attempting to live a life grounded in Godliness.

Questions:

1. What have you done or are doing that may make God "sick"?
2. What steps can you take to be more "appetizing" in the sight of the Lord and less "sickening"?

Prayer:

Father, I confess my sins to you today. Forgive me for each and every sin that I may have committed knowingly or unknowingly that may have made you "sick". Give me the strength to not commit those sins again. I recognize that you want to prosper me, and I cannot prosper and be well with the infection of sin. I declare that I am reborn, free of the sickness of sin. In Jesus` name I pray. Amen.

TURN AWAY AND PRAY

Numbers 20:5-6

Day 4

Numbers 20: 5-6, *Good News Translation*

- *Why did you make us leave Egypt and bring us here to this terrible place? This land has no grain, no figs, no grapes, no pomegranates, and no water to drink!" Moses and Aaron turned away from the people and went to the entrance of the Tabernacle, where they fell face down on the ground. Then the glorious presence of the Lord appeared to them...*

Complaints. We all get them. We all give them: weather, traffic, Mondays, customer service, youth. And don`t forget, we complain about people who complain, too. It is notorious that all workspaces have a "Negative Nancy" or a "Downer Dan"—individuals who embody pessimism and frequently complain about even the slightest things. These individuals burden others with complaints, typically using said complaints as a means to fuel an intolerable, discordant, and even dysfunctional work environment.

I recall when I was in high school it was customary to tell adults "good morning" upon seeing them. I remember one morning walking into class and telling my English teacher, "Good morning", to which she replied, "What's good about it?" Not knowing how to respond, I remained quiet. I now know the answer. What's good about it, you ask? What's good about it is that God woke us up this morning, what's good about it is that his mercies are new every day; what's good about it is that he allowed us to get to school safely; what's good about it is he allowed us to function in a right state of mind, what's good about it is today is another chance for us to get life right; what's good about it is because Jesus chose to lay down his life, he allowed us to get up and for that we must not utter a complaint.

Many individuals reference Numbers chapter 20 as a means to share the story of how God miraculously allowed water to flow from a rock after the Israelites demanded thirst as they traversed the wilderness, passing through Zin. The Israelites grew frustrated as they faced famine, lack of water, battle and other hardship; they frequently complained to Moses and Aaron crying and pleading about why they couldn't have just died instead of being led to the wilderness with no grain, figs, grapes, pomegranates, and water. These instances are recorded as the Seven Rebellions, or instances where the Israelites complain and rebel. Moses and Aaron had had enough of their complaints, but notice their posture and response in verse six, following yet another Israelite complaint. Scripture states, "Moses and Aaron turned away from the people and went to the entrance of the Tabernacle, where they fell face down on the ground" (Numbers 20: 6, Good News Translation). Moses and Aaron did not argue, fuss, fight, or retaliate; they simply turned away, and prayed.

People in our lives can get us so worked up, causing us to reach our breaking points that we feel the urge to retaliate through argument, swearing, fighting or a combination of these and others. But God shows us in Scripture that despite the urge to respond, it is simply best to turn away and pray for it is the Lord who will provide us direction and the peace we need to get through even the hardest days. Don`t respond: turn away and pray!

Questions:

1. What do you often find yourself complaining about?
2. To whom do you often complain? How might they feel about your complaints?
3. How can you exhibit a "turn away and pray" mentality through all of life's hardships despite wanting to respond reactively?

Prayer:

Father, help me to see the brighter side in all situations. Do not allow me to dwell in complaining, but rather strengthen me to turn my complaints into contentment and turn my thoughts of pessimism into moments of prayer. Help me to be grateful in all hardship for you are the author and finisher of all things and have my entire life in your hands. In Jesus` name I pray. Amen.

REMEMBER ME

Deuteronomy 8:18

Day 5

Deuteronomy 8: 18, *New International Version*

- *But remember the Lord your God...*

"Don`t forget where you came from" is a common quote one hears repeatedly, often when the recipient of the quote is acting in a pretentious manner or boasting about some form of newfound success. The quote is intended to redirect one`s mindset by helping one realize that they did not reach success on their own, and that one's roots, background, and upbringing helped shape that individual into their success. I want to encourage you today to not ask yourself where you came from, but *who* you came from: our Father, which art in heaven. Yes, we may have been physically and naturally conceived by our maternal figure, but it is our Lord who birthed and created us over 2,000 years ago. Remember him, for it is he and he alone who is solely responsible for who you are at this moment in time.

In Deuteronomy 8, Moses is reminding the Israelites of the good things the Lord has done for them on this journey: "leading them through the wilderness for forty years, feeding them manna, keeping their clothes in good condition, disciplining them, and protecting them from snakes and scorpions (Deuteronomy 8, New International Version). Moses then assures the Israelites of the promise, reminding them that it is God whom they should remember for delivering them thus far. Moses writes, "Be careful that you do not forget the Lord your God...when you eat and are satisfied, when you build fine houses and settle down, when your herds and flocks grow large and your silver and gold multiply" (Deuteronomy 8, New International Version). Moses concludes by stating, "You may say to yourself, "My power and the strength of my hands have reproduced this wealth for me", but remember the Lord your God, for it is he who gives you the ability to produce wealth" (Deuteronomy 8: 17-18, New International Version).

When we succeed in life in big ways or small, we often believe that we`ve reached success on our own. While we pay little recognition to *where* we`ve come, we sometimes pay even less recognition to *who* we came from: the Lord. We may think that our "hands" have allowed us to get this career, or this home, or this land, or these expensive items, but truly if it had not been for the Lord's hands, we'd have none of what we have today. The person worthy of giving credit to concerning ourselves and our lives is the Lord. "Everything came into existence through him. Not one thing that exists was made without him" (John 1:3, God's Word Translation). Without God, we are nothing for he deserves all the glory, the honor, and the praise for making us who we are. Remember him!

Questions:

1. How often do you give yourself credit or pat yourself on the back for "wins" you experience?
2. What are some "wins" for which you can give the Lord credit today?
3. What can you do routinely to remember God, giving him credit in all things?

Prayer:

Father, help me to change my "I`s" to "you`s": not look at what *I* did, but look at what *you* did, Lord. Help me to remember you in all circumstances: both good and bad. Lord, I ask that as I transition from a time of "wilderness" where I seem lost and uncertain and begin to walk into my promised land of abundance and prosperity, that you will allow me to remember you and give you all the credit, glory, honor, and praise. In Jesus` name I pray. Amen.

SHAME TO FAME

Joshua 6:25

Day 6

Joshua 6:25, *Good News Translation*

- *But Joshua spared the lives of the prostitute Rahab and all her relatives, because she had hidden the two spies that he had sent to Jericho. (Her descendants have lived in Israel to this day.)*

If your past could speak, what might it tell? Would it speak of adultery? Arrogance? Disobedience? Would it speak of drunkenness? Envy? Lust? Would it speak of homosexuality? Idolatry? Prostitution? Would it speak all of the above, none of the above, or a combination of these amongst other sins? How much power do you give your past to speak ill of your shortcomings, your mistakes, your sins, your biggest disappointments, let-downs, or issues you have with yourself? While your past may not be something you can alter, erase, revise or rectify, it has made you the person you are today. Be thankful for your past—all of it. Don`t leave any of it out. Declare today that that past hurt, pain, and shame will lead to your road to fame for the bible teaches "for those who love God all things work together for good, for those who are called according to his purpose (Romans 8:28, English Standard Version). Let God use your shame for fame, for it is *all* for your good.

As the Israelites grew closer to the Promised Land after traversing 40 years in the wilderness led by Moses, God appointed Joshua (one of Moses` assistants) to lead the Israelites to the Promised Land. To prepare for their arrival, Joshua sends two spies to Jericho; the two men were led to the house of a prostitute named Rahab. Rahab, having heard of the glorious things the Lord did for the Israelites during their travels, revered and respected God, leading her to hide the men from the king of Jericho, who searched for them. In exchange for their concealment, Rahab asked the two spies to protect her and her family after the Israelites conquer Jericho. The spies informed Joshua of their promise and in Joshua 6 after conquering Jericho, Joshua commands the spies to find Rahab (a prostitute) and her family and keep the promise they had vowed to her, to which Scripture informs us that Rahab and *all* her relatives had been spared. Rahab and her family were the only ones spared from the conquering of the city.

Rahab (a prostitute). A prostitute. A *prostitute*. While readers are uncertain about how Rahab felt concerning her profession of prostitution, I can imagine the amount of people who looked down at her in shame. But don`t you know we serve a God who can transform our shame to bring us fame? While the bible is filled with so many individuals who committed shameful acts (Jacob was a cheater; Peter had a temper; David had an affair; Noah got drunk, Paul was a murderer; Thomas was a doubter; Jonah ran from God), we serve a God that doesn't call the qualified, he qualifies the called by giving us fame despite our shame. Being the only survivors from Jericho in a land now accompanied by Israelites, I can only imagine the fame Rahab and her family possessed. Notice that not just was Rahab protected, but her entire family. Don't be ashamed of your past, for God is going to put your past to shame and bring fame and favor not only to you, but everyone attached to you as well. No matter the shame of your past, remember that we are royalty, children of the King; therefore, we can't be stripped of our title, our royalty, our calling, our assignment, or even our favor because of the shame of our past. Let go of your past, accept who you are because of it, and let God turn your shame into fame!

Questions:

1. What have you done in your past that makes you feel ashamed or embarrassed?
2. How do you cope with this shame and/or embarrassment? Is the coping mechanism healthy?
3. Despite your past mistakes, God still gives you purpose (just like he did Rahab, the prostitute). How does knowing and living in your purpose help you to overcome past shame and/or embarrassment?

Prayer:

Father, direct me in my purpose. Allow me to realize that despite my past mistakes, sins, and even embarrassments that you can still use me for your glory for I have a divine purpose, gift, and assignment that will prevail no matter the shame of my past. I declare today that I am turning my shame into fame for I am a child of the king and am therefore, a product of royalty. In Jesus` name I pray. Amen.

SERVING WITHOUT SEEING

Judges 2:7

Day 7

Judges 2:7, *English Standard Version*

- *And the people served the Lord all the days of Joshua, and all the days of the elders who outlived Joshua, who had seen all the great work that the Lord had done for Israel.*

What does it mean to serve? To whom or what do you serve? What does it look like to serve? Merriam-Webster dictionary defines the verb "serve" simply as "being of use [to someone]." Biblically speaking, to serve essentially means to align ourselves with God by following his will and doing what he commands us to do. What I find interesting is that how I serve God may not be how you serve God. Serving can take different forms. Think about it. In any given church organization, you can have bishops, elders, pastors, deacons and deaconesses, ushers, stewards, trustees, sextons, singers etc. Although each of their roles and responsibilities are different, they still serve one God—in their own capacities. Likewise in a restaurant, you may have distinct roles such as servers, cooks, runners, bussers, hosts and hostesses, dishwashers, cashiers, and even management who all serve you, the customer! What is interesting is that while you may only come in physical contact or sight with a few of these roles, they all serve you. Their physical sight of the customer is not tied to their willingness to serve. The Israelites were not aware of this revelation.

Joshua, who was now tasked with leading the Israelites to the Promised Land, knew of his impending death. Joshua addressed the Israelites saying, "...fear the Lord and serve him in sincerity and in faithfulness. Put away the gods (idols) that your fathers served beyond the River and in Egypt, and serve the Lord" (Joshua 24:14). One of God's commandments discusses not serving idols, but only serving God. Note that idols do not necessarily have to be human; they can be materialistic or even abstract: homes, land, money, promotion, power, status etc. The Israelites fell back into sin as Judges 2:7 states, "And the people served the Lord all the days of Joshua, and all the days of the elders who outlived Joshua, who had seen all the great work that the Lord had done for Israel" (Judges 1:7, English Standard Version). Scripture later states, "And there arose another generation after them who did not know the Lord or the work that he had done for Israel and the people of Israel did what was evil in the sight of the Lord..." (Judges 2: 10-11). In other words, the *only* Israelites who served the Lord were the ones who physically saw what he did; on the contrary, those who did not see the great works of the Lord in the wilderness, chose not to serve him, meaning their serving was only tied to their sight—what they physically saw or currently see the Lord do.

Is your serving tied to your sight? Just because you can't see the Lord, does not mean he should not be served. God is omnipotent, omnipresent, and omniscience therefore we cannot hide from him. Just because we cannot physically see God, does not mean he cannot see us. School custodians do not see all the students for whom they clean, yet they still serve. Cooks do not see the customers for every dish they prepare, yet they still serve. Congressmen and congresswomen do not see all whom a law affects, yet they still serve. You do not see everyone you impact, yet you must still serve. Serve God although you cannot see him, for he sees you, hears you, and is in control.

Questions:

1. Who do you serve?
2. How do you serve?
3. How often do you serve?
4. How can you serve God, although you can't physically see him?

Prayer:

Father, help me to serve you daily, although I cannot see you. Although I cannot see you, help me to feel your presence each and every day, giving gentle reminders that you never leave my side. Guide me in serving you and show me how I can better serve others in my walk with you. In Jesus` name I pray. Amen.

FAITH TO FAVOR

Ruth 2:12

Day 8

Ruth 2: 12, *English Standard Version*

- *The Lord repay you for what you have done, and a full reward be given you by the Lord, the God of Israel, under whose wings you have come to take refuge!"*

1. Are you bold enough to *think* that God owes you? 2. Are you bold enough to *believe* that God owes you? 3. Are you bold enough to *voice* that God owes you? 4. Are you bold enough to *tell* God that he owes you? As you read that series of questions, what question—one, two, three, or four—made you squirm, feel uncomfortable, or even feel audacious? Why? Each question was intentionally written with a stronger verb each time, requiring a response of "yes" or "no." For me, I started squirming at question one and felt completely and utterly audacious at the conclusion of question four. Why? Because God owes us nothing! Job 41:11 writes, "Who has first given to me, that I should repay him? Whatever is under the whole heaven is mine" (English Standard Version). Although God owes us nothing, it doesn't mean he is not able to repay us. "Repay us for what?" you ask. Our faithfulness.

In the book of Ruth, the Israelites are still being led or ruled by various judges as a famine struck the land. We meet a couple named Elimelech and Naomi who have two sons named Mahlon and Chilion who marry two Moabite women: one named Orpah and the other named Ruth. As time passed, Elimelech (husband of Naomi), along with Mahlon and Chilion (sons of Naomi) died, leaving Naomi with her daughters-in-law, Ruth and Orpah. After persuading Ruth and Orpah to return to their mother`s houses, Orpah obeyed reluctantly, but Ruth remained loyal to Naomi and the two navigated to Bethlehem. Although Ruth was a Moab (a people with a troubling relationship with Israel), she remained faithful to Naomi by going with her to Bethlehem. While there, Ruth meets a man named Boaz who allows her to "glean among the ears of grain" to which Ruth declares "in whose sight I shall find favor" (Ruth 2:2, English Standard Version), and Boaz did just that as she was given access to the harvest, and later an inheritance. Ruth asks Boaz, "Why have I found favor in your eyes, that you should take notice of me, since I am a foreigner?" He responds, "The Lord repay you for what you have done, and a full reward be given you by the Lord, the God of Israel, under whose wings you have come to take refuge! (Ruth 2:12, English Standard Version). Not only did Boaz ask the Lord to simply repay Ruth, but the bible says, "*and* a full reward be given." *And*, meaning in addition to! Not only will God repay you to your faithfulness, but he will give you "ands" as well—repayment *and* favor, repayment *and* prosperity; repayment *and* increase—just as he did Ruth.

Ruth's faithfulness to Naomi was rewarded due to her sacrifice, leading her to find favor in Boaz. Note that the term used here is "faithfulness" as loyalty is conditional, meaning one can be loyal to someone or something as long as their needs are being met. Naomi had nothing—no family, no money, no food—displaying the true faith of Ruth, leading to her favor. While Ruth was faithful to Naomi she *still* received repayment *and* an additional reward from God. Imagine what your faithfulness to God (and not man) will pay you. While I am unaware of where you are in your walk of faith, I suggest putting your faith in the Lord to turn your faith into favor.

Questions:

1. What does faith mean to you?
2. To whom or what do you place your faith?
3. How can you remain faithful (not loyal) to the Lord of your salvation?
4. What is your vision or meaning of favor? How can you receive it?

Prayer:

Father, help me to remain faithful to you. I realize that my faith in you is not conditional and should not be based on life`s ups and downs, but should remain constant as your love for me remains constant. While I am a sinner, help me to find favor in your sight due to my unwavering faith in you. In Jesus` name I pray. Amen.

'

CAN YOU HEAR ME NOW?

1 Samuel 1:13

Day 9

1 Samuel 1:13, *Holman Christian Standard Bible*

- *While she continued praying in the Lord's presence, Eli watched her lips. Hannah was praying silently, and though her lips were moving, her voice could not be heard. Eli thought she was drunk*

There are typically three to four questions we ask someone when determining which mobile phone company to sign up with. The first of these questions is, "What kind of phone do you have?" We generally ask this question to see how well the next person is doing technologically speaking to get a feel for about how much we might spend if we switch to that phone company. The second question we normally ask is "Who is your carrier?" We ask this question to determine if we should continue our interrogation process because we know Verizon`s quality isn't every carrier`s quality. Our third question is usually "How much do you pay a month?" and our last, yet most important question is, "Do you get good service?" In other words, we are trying to find out whether or not this mobile phone carrier will allow us to make and receive calls clearly no matter where we go. A few issues we have with cell phone service these days is we can't understand the other person on the line, or we can`t hear well and most of the time it is due to our location. Oftentimes when we are near a school, under a shaded area blocked with trees, in bad weather, in an elevator, on a plane, or even sometimes in schools or government-run businesses and organizations we find difficulty in establishing a good service connection and find ourselves asking the question, "Can you hear me now?"

In the book of 1st Samuel, we depart temporarily from the biblical narrative and meet a man named Elkanah who had two wives: Peninnah and Hannah. Peninnah had children, but Hannah did not; because of her inability to have children, Peninnah would taunt and make fun of Hannah. This act occurred for years, causing Hannah on several occasions to cry or even refuse to eat. Hannah went to the Tabernacle and made a vow to the Lord pleading, "Lord, if you will look upon my sorrow and answer my prayer and give me a son, then I will give him back to you" (1 Samuel 1:11). Eli, the priest, watched her pray and assumed Hannah was drunk because all he could see was her mouth moving with no sound coming out. In other words, her prayer to the Lord was silent, yet we discover later that the Lord granted her request: "and in due time she gave birth to a son, naming him Samuel (1 Samuel 1:20, New Living Translation).

Notice that Hannah`s prayer was silent, yet the Lord heard and answered her prayer. Although mankind can`t hear what we utter in silence, the Lord can. I can imagine in all her nights of praying and weeping, Hannah asked the question countless times, "Lord, can you hear me now?" This story shows us that even when we do not voice a word, the Lord knows our heart, hears our prayers, and will act on his time and not ours. Do you ever pray for something so persistently, you begin to ask God "Can you hear me now?" I`ve come to tell you as long as you`ve got God, you`ve got good service and he can hear you clearly. He can hear you now; he could hear you then; he can hear you in the future; and he can even hear you before you even begin to speak. His service plan called prayer has no feedback, no static, no service charge, the line does not go dead, does not go offline, does not drop the call, does not search for service, does not lose signal strength, does not lose charge, does not "go in and out", and does not lose reception no matter where you are or when you call. Before you even open your mouth to talk to God, trust and believe he knows, he hears, and he answers prayers. Delay is not denial. He may not come when you want him, but he is always on time. Believe it!

Questions:
1. What is one thing for which you have asked God for persistently?
2. How long have you been waiting for an answer or a result?
3. What can you do to not lose faith or grow impatient in your period of waiting for God to deliver?

Prayer:

Lord, help me to be patient in my waiting. Help me to understand that although you do not answer prayer as I see fit, that you orchestrate time so perfectly. I realize that a blessing too soon is not a blessing at all. Give me the strength to wait, the faith to believe, and the ability to receive all you have for me in due timing. In Jesus` name I pray. Amen.

A COLD SHOWER OR A DISPLEASING BATH?

2 Samuel 11:27

Day 10

---

2 Samuel 11:27, *New International Version*

- *But the thing David had done displeased the Lord.*

Sin. Sexual sin. A topic no one wants to talk about, but one in which many indulge. While I may have the least knowledge in this social aspect of life, I do know what Scripture states and implies concerning sexual sin. Sexual sin is defined as not obeying the parameters for which the Lord placed concerning sexual relations between people: homosexuality, lesbianism, prostitution, rape, fornication, adultery, lust, or even incest. Yes, it may be difficult to stave off sexual energy, but we all have to find that "cold shower" to help us remain sexually pure. While it may not eliminate the desire completely, it does or could help one refrain from sexual sin. Scripture teaches, "For this is the will of God, your sanctification: that you abstain from sexual immorality; that each one of you know how to control his own body in holiness and honor, not in the passion of lust just like the Gentiles who do not know God" (1 Thessalonians 4:3-5, English Standard Version).

In Samuel 2, we are presented with Samuel—Israel's next judge. God grants Samuel permission to appoint a king, leading to the appointment of Saul as king. Because Saul disobeyed God, God allowed Samuel to elect a new king: David. Saul grew jealous of David and tried various attempts to kill him, but his efforts were to no avail. Saul later died in battle and David unified the kingdoms of Israel and Judah, residing as king over Israel. David began his rise to power, conquering cities, expanding borders, and developing relations with neighboring kingdoms. David also had many wives. One day while roaming his rooftop, David saw a woman named Bathsheba bathing, who was married to a man named Uriah. David sent messengers to get Bathsheba and he slept with her; she later became pregnant. David tried many tactics to rid Uriah, ultimately writing a letter that caused Uriah to be placed on the front lines of battle, leading to his unfortunate, yet honorable death. Bathsheba did conceive a child, but the bible writes, "...the thing David had done displeased the Lord" (2 Samuel 11:27). In other words, instead of taking a "cold shower", David chose to take a displeasing bath, soaking in sexual sin by sleeping with Bathsheba.

The key word in this verse is "done", meaning it was an action or a choice that caused David to sin. In our daily lives we face many choices, specifically sexual choices despite our status (single, married, divorced, unmarried, widowed) or even sexual orientation. Yet, so many times we decide to take a bath or a displeasing dive (in the eyes of the Lord) in sexual sin. For those of you who may have a past or a current desire to indulge in sexual sin, you should identify what your "cold shower" is—that thing that will prevent you from succumbing to sexual immorality.

Questions:
1. Have you committed or are committing acts of sexual sin?
2. What can you establish as your "cold shower" to avoid sexual sin?

Prayer:
Lord, relieve me of any sexual desires that are immoral in your sight. Give me strength to rise above those desires as I seek a walk of Godliness as I draw closer to you. In Jesus` name I pray. Amen.

INTENTIONAL ASKING

1 Kings 3:5

Day 11

---

1 Kings 3:5, *New Living Translation*

- *That night the Lord appeared to Solomon in a dream, and God said, "What do you want? Ask, and I will give it to you!"*

What do you want? This question may be deemed a loaded question that people tend to answer impetuously. If God revealed himself to you and asked you personally and in an inoffensive manner, "What do you want?" how might you respond? Popular answers would probably include money, cars, a certain career or promotion, influence, or even some fine jewelry. Others might ask for a miracle for a loved one in need or healing for a broken world. Another might even be so led to ask for more "wishes"—missing out on the opportunity because of indecisiveness. The verb "want" describes a yearning or desire for something—often a desire we have in the moment. What if God were to ask you, "What do you *need*?" Would your answer be similar to your wants? "Need" is a verb that describes something one has to depend on heavily as a means to not just survive but thrive.

2nd Samuel closes with many failed attempts of King David`s child, Absalom, trying to take the throne. Absalom was later killed as Judah and Israel were later united under the rightful rule of King David. 1 Kings opens with an introduction to David, who is now old and bedridden. His son, Adonijah, unrightfully takes the throne, but David appoints Solomon (son of David and Bathsheba) as king. Solomon, knowing the fickle state of the Israelites, knew that being king would be a challenging task. Solomon was a symbol of obedience for the Lord, leading to the Lord appearing to him in a dream asking, "What do you want?" Solomon, recognizing the charge of leadership before him, responded, "I am like a little child who doesn't know his way around. And here I am in the midst of your own chosen people, a nation so great and numerous they cannot be counted" (1 Kings 3:7-8, New Living Translation), two things representative of a grand kingdom: status (chosen people) and size (a population too large to be counted). Solomon could have taken the easy way out asking for a smaller kingdom, more leadership, or even a new king; he could have been avaricious, asking for more power, more people, or even a greater palace. Of the countless things Solomon could have asked for, he chose to ask for wisdom. Wisdom not to defeat his enemies, wisdom not to manipulate people, wisdom not to be used for negative gain, wisdom not to boast or brag, but wisdom to "to rule your [God`s] people with justice and to know the difference between good and evil" (1 Kings 3:9, Good News Translation). And because Solomon coupled a wish with intention, God granted his wish, giving him more wisdom, understanding, and discernment that no one else in the bible possessed.

It is common to ask God for things we need and want, but if our petition is not coupled with the appropriate intention, then what we ask God for is simply in vain. Solomon`s decision teaches us two things: to be specific for what it is that we ask from God *and* to be intentional in our asking. We can ask God for a spouse, but if we do not put specific parameters on what we`re asking for nor have the godly intentions, we may not get what we want and begin to falsely blame God for what we receive. While the Lord hears our requests, the devil keeps his ears open for loopholes in our requests just so when we get what we ask for, we get angry at the Lord and turn away from him. The bible teaches that "life and death are in the power of the tongue" (Proverbs 18:21, King James Version). Speak things into existence. Ask God for what you want and need but ensure that you are specific in your request and have the right intentions. The right intention triggers God's attention.

Questions:
1. What do you ask of God?
2. What do you want from the Lord? What is your intention?
3. What do you need from the Lord? What is your intention?

Prayer:
Father: Help me to be more conscious of the things for which I ask of you. Help me to align my intentions to your will in my life. Grant me the wisdom and discernment of Solomon to ask for that which will help me and not hinder. I thank you this day for answered and unanswered prayers for I realize that if I received it, it was meant for me and if I didn`t, it was also meant for me. Lord, I love you and I thank you. In Jesus` name I pray. Amen.

IT'S TIME TO CLEAN HOUSE

2 Kings 23:3

Day 12

---

2 Kings 23:3, *New Living Translation*

- *The king took his place of authority beside the pillar and renewed the covenant in the Lord's presence. He pledged to obey the Lord by keeping all his commands, laws, and decrees with all his heart and soul. In this way, he confirmed all the terms of the covenant that were written in the scroll, and all the people pledged themselves to the covenant.*

In the year 2016, Donald Trump was elected the 45th president of the United States. While not necessarily being one of the things Donald Trump ran on, it is evident that Donald Trump drastically changed government personnel. Headlines ranging from "President Trump was Elected to Clean House" and "Trump Cleaning House, Teasing New Leadership for Top Intel Agency" reflect the major personnel changes of the Trump presidency. Even more fascinating, Trump set the record, having the greatest turnover rate in the first year of his administration in all presidents of American history. The term "cleaning house" in its non-literal sense refers to the idea of removing or eliminating all inefficiency and ineffectiveness within an organization in hopes of renewing or revamping the core of the organization for improvement. "Cleaning house" can refer to your home by tossing things you no longer need or want; the phrase can refer to your circle of friends by getting rid of those who do not benefit you; the phrase can even refer to yourself by ridding qualities that do not enhance your character. It's time to clean house!

In 2nd Kings we follow the royal lineage beginning with Solomon, a king—who because of his wish—lived in opulence: wealth, a grand palace, a large empire, longevity, and fame. Solomon grew overzealous, marrying women who influenced him to worship idols. Solomon dies, causing his son Rehoboam to assume the throne. As time went on, Israel`s kings became more disobedient, more heartless, and more unfaithful to God (with the exception of few), leading to the removal of God's presence with the people of Israel. In 2 Kings 23 we are introduced to King Josiah. Josiah exhibited the "clean house" leadership mentality as he recognized that the Israelites have, yet again, succumbed to worshiping idols, losing their favor from the Lord. Josiah removed all the articles used to worship idols, fired the idolatrous priests, tore down living quarters of prostitutes, demolished and burned pagan buildings, shrines, altars and statues, and rid every detestable practice that was not of God.

Finally, Josiah reinstated the Passover since such a celebration had not occurred since the judges ruled Israel. Scripture writes, "Never before had there been a king like Josiah, who turned to the Lord with all his heart, soul, and strength, obeying the law of Moses. And there has never been a king like him since" (2 Kings 3:25, New Living Translation). Josiah "cleaned house" and renewed the covenant with the Lord.

How can you renew your "house" with the Lord? Sometimes we have to rid everything that is not of God so that we can make room for his presence. I remember specifically near the end of the year 2022, I felt like I was simply on autopilot, seeming as if my spiritual life had become so formulaic and mundane that I was missing something. I had to clean house, making room for more fervent praying, deliberate fasting, close reading of the Word, and more genuine loving to myself and others. As believers we often get so content with God that we give him the bare minimum, using grace as the only insurance to keep our "house" protected. Isaac Carree wrote a song called "Clean My House" in which he writes, "Clean this house from the inside out/ Restore me, take away my impurity" (Carree). God is truly the best cleaner alive for he can rid sin, rid mistakes, rid strongholds, rid demons, rid toxicity, rid negativity, and rid you from anything that makes your "house" not like him. It's time to clean house. Invite the Lord in for he charges no fee. He`ll clean your "house" up for free, renewing a right spirit within you *for* him.

Questions:
1. What in your "house" (total self) needs to be cleaned?
2. How do these things not serve or benefit you?
3. What is your expectation for being renewed? In other words, what do you want to see in your renewal?
4. How can you or will you renew your relationship with the Lord daily?

Prayer:
Father: Rid me of all things that are not of you. Help me to lead a life with a "clean house", making more room for you daily. Lord, I ask that you find in your will to move into my heart and my home and take permanent residence with me so that I can be renewed daily. In Jesus` name I pray. Amen.

WHAT DOES GOD SEE IN YOU?

1 Chronicles 2:3

Day 13

---

1 Chronicles 2:3, *New International Version*

- *The sons of Judah: Er, Onan and Shelah. These three were born to him by a Canaanite woman, the daughter of Shua. Er, Judah's firstborn, was wicked in the Lord's sight; so the Lord put him to death.*

In our more intimate relationships with our partners, the question "What do you see in me?" tends to be the foundational question *and* answer for the relationship. Essentially, each party wants to know the qualities that attract them to one another. While such qualities (whether positive or negative) are fundamental and lay the groundwork for relationships, have you ever thought to ask yourself what God sees in you? This question goes beyond the biblical responses of him seeing us as his sons and daughters, as his child or friend, as conquerors or even as his creation; the commonality in this list is that these are all nouns: sons, daughters, child, friend, conqueror, creation. What God truly sees and judges us by is beyond these nouns, but are our adjectives—qualities that describe our innate and genuine identity. For example, one may deem their significant others as a wife, husband, friend, mother, father, breadwinner, protector, or even by their job title; but the true determinant of what someone sees in you is not by the nouns that describe you, but by the adjectives that comprise you. What does God see in you?

Although the author of 1 and 2 Chronicles is anonymous, the books rely on books and records to produce its content. These two books mirror 2 Samuel and 1 Kings as it focuses on David's reign. One of the biggest aspects of 1 Chronicles is its genealogies, which offer the legitimacy of a person or family's claim to a leadership role, in this case, that of who is leading the chosen people (of Israel and Judah), despite the peoples' fickle character. Near the end of 1 Chronicles, we learn that "Satan rose up against Israel and caused David to take a census of the people..." (1 Chronicles 21:1, New Living Translation), which displeased the Lord, sending a plague upon Israel. David was instructed to build an altar, later giving instructions for Solomon to build a Temple. At the opening of 1 Chronicles, we meet the sons of Judah (Er, Onan, and Shelah), but the bible says, "Er, Judah's firstborn, was wicked in the Lord's sight, so the Lord put him to death." Because the Lord saw wickedness in Er's heart, he was sentenced to damnation. However, on the contrary one finds that near the closing of 1 Chronicles, David offers Solomon, his succession to the throne, some wisdom: "...know the

God of your ancestors intimately. Worship and serve him with your whole heart and a willing mind. For the Lord *sees* every heart and knows every plan and thought. If you seek him, you will find him. But if you forsake him, he will reject you forever" (1 Chronicles 28:9, New Living Translation). Under Solomon's rule, this Temple—the *Lord's* temple—was one of the most notable and magnificent pieces of architecture in all the bible, simply because God *saw* Solomon`s heart: a heart of servitude, willingness, wisdom, and righteousness.

What does God see when he sees you? Does he see wickedness or willingness? Does he see haughtiness or humbleness? Does he see lust or love; jealousy or joy; pessimism or peacefulness; fickleness or faithfulness; selfishness or self-control? What does God see in you? What is so amazing about God is that he is so gracious that he allows us the ability to change the adjectives we associate with our name. What you will find is that as you begin to change your adjectives, that you will begin to form that intimate (up close and personal) relationship with the Lord so he can see you as you want to be seen. He won't see you as man sees you for man is surely to find fault; but God sees you with perfect vision, uniquely and wonderfully made in his hands.

Questions:
1. What does God see in you?
2. What do you want God to see in you?
3. What can you do daily to allow God to see you this way?

Prayer:
Lord, help me to find favor in your sight. Remove anything in me that is not of you. I want you to see me as one who whole-heartedly represents your fruit of the spirit. Give me more love, more joy, more peace, more patience, more kindness, more goodness, more faithfulness, more gentleness, more self-control, more you. Help me to see me as I see you. Lord, I love you and thank you. In Jesus` name I pray. Amen.

YOUR PRAISE IS MIGHTIER THAN YOUR SWORD

2 Chronicles 20:22

Day 14

---

2 Chronicles 20:22, *New Living Translation*

- *At the very moment they began to sing and give praise, the Lord caused the armies of Ammon, Moab, and Mount Seir to start fighting among themselves.*

In 1839, playwright Edward Bulwer-Lytton coined the phrase "the pen is mightier than the sword." In layman's terms, this quote expresses the idea that writing or even our voices are more effective and more potent than violence. Similarly, Langston Hughes wrote a poem that demonstrates the power of words called "Little Old Letter". He writes, "It was yesterday morning/ I looked in my box for my mail./ The letter that I found there/ Made me turn right pale. / Just a little old letter, / wasn't even one page long— / But it made me wish / I was in my grave: and gone. / Just a pencil and paper, / You don't need no gun nor knife—/ A little old letter / Can take a person's life." The poem, though simply written, shows the disastrous effects words can have on people. Yes, sticks and stones may hurt, but words can hurt even harder. Words do hurt. There is power in our tongue to speak life or death in our lives and others, but did you know that you have even greater power in your praise? Your praise is mightier than your sword.

2 Chronicles spans from the period of Solomon`s ascension to the throne until Judah's exile in Babylon. After the temple was built for the Lord using the plans given to David from the Lord, the unified kingdom of Judah and Israel split under the rule of Rehoboam, Solomon`s son. From then on, the kingdom witnessed many kings, both righteous and unrighteous. 2 Chronicles 17-21 is dedicated to the reign of Jehoshaphat, the fourth king of Judah. In the 20th chapter, Jehoshaphat just received word that the Moabites, Ammonites, and Meunites have declared war on Jehoshaphat, leading to Jehoshaphat begging the Lord for guidance, ordering the people of Judah to fast and calling a prayer meeting with all the people of Judah. The Spirit of the Lord descended as Jahaziel (son of Zechariah) uttered, "This is what the Lord says: do not be afraid, for the battle is not yours, but God`s. You will not even need to fight. Take your positions; then stand still and watch the Lord`s victory" (2 Chronicles 20:15-17, New Living Translation). Jehoshaphat led the kingdom in prayer and on the following morning as the army marched to the place of battle, Jehoshaphat "appointed singers to walk ahead of the army, singing to the Lord and praising his holy splendor" (2 Chronicles 20:21, New Living Translation). Scripture continues, "At the

very moment they began to sing and give praise, the Lord caused the armies of Ammon, Moab, and Mount Seir to start fighting amongst themselves, destroying themselves, attacking each other. When the army of Judah arrived, all they saw were dead bodies lying on the ground. Not a single one of the enemy had escaped" (2 Chronicles 20:22-24, New Living Translation).

What is so encouraging is that Jehoshaphat's army did not have to lift a finger to fight; their praise proved mightier than any sword or weapon they had brought with them. The Lord allowed the enemy to turn on themselves, killing each other before the battle had even begun. I challenge you that no matter the battles you face in your life whether it be battles of anxiety or depression, battles of health issues or trauma, battles of financial burdens or debt, battles of unbelief or sadness, or even battles of toxic friends and family, all you need to do is praise the Lord in advance for he will give you the victory. Don't carry any weapons or worry, don't carry any artillery or motive, don't carry any schemes or tactics, all you need is the power of your praise to prove you the prizewinner. Notice Jehoshaphat did not let the warriors lead the battle, but rather he put the "choir" on the front line. No military man or woman would decide to lead a platoon with praisers on the front line, but through this tactic, Jehoshaphat proved that the power of praise is potent. Your praise is mightier than your sword. The battle is not yours, it's the Lord`s. Pray, sit back, and let God earn you the victory!

Questions:
1. What does it mean to "praise God?"
2. How do you praise God?
3. How can you shift your praise to being more proactive and less reactive?

Prayer:
Lord, you are enough. Help my mouth to be filled with your praise in all circumstances. I realize Lord that there are battles in my life that I cannot fight alone; but all I need to do is praise you for my praise is mightier than any sword. Give me the strength and reassurance to believe in you, your word, your will, and your way so you can fight my battles each and every day. In Jesus` name I pray. Amen.

TEAMWORK MAKES THE DREAMWORK

Ezra 3:8

Day 15

Ezra 3:8, *New Living Translation*

- *The construction of the Temple of God began in mid spring, during the second year after they arrived in Jerusalem. The work force was made up of everyone who had returned from exile...*

On April 3, 2002, John C. Maxwell published a book called "Teamwork Makes the Dream Work." The premise of the book was for individuals to understand and be receptive to the fact that working as a team could help one fulfill their dreams. "Teams" in this case do not simply refer to sports teams, but also relate to spouses in marriage, colleagues at work, or even volunteers for a cause. While this cliche is catchy and memorable, let's admit that working together does not always yield the best results; further, teamwork is not successful 100% of the time. While Maxwell makes specific references to marriage, colleagues, and volunteers, I choose to extend this interpretation to the body of Christ for the bible teaches, "The human body has many parts, but the many parts make up one whole body. So it is with the body of Christ. Some of us are Jews, some are Gentiles, some are slaves, and some are free. But we have all been baptized into one body by one Spirit" (1 Corinthians 12:12-13, New Living Translation). The bible continues, "All of you together are Christ's body, and each of you is a part of it" (1 Corinthians 12:27, New Living Translation). We are one!

The book of Ezra picks up following Judah's exile in Babylon after their continued disobedience to the Lord. Ezra was a prominent figure in leading exiled Jews from Babylon to Jerusalem and surrounding areas. As the exiled Jews traveled to Jerusalem, they—along with men, priests, Levites, servants, descendants of kings, singers, and gatekeepers—all worked together to unify themselves and restore the temple. The bible states, "The construction of the Temple of God began in mid-spring, during the second year after they arrived in Jerusalem. The workforce was made up of everyone who had returned from exile" (Ezra 3:8, New Living Translation). Notice, the bible uses the term "everyone" to show the collective effort needed to restore the temple. In other words, it took teamwork to make the dreamwork. What I find so interesting is that not only did it take folks of lower status (servants, gatekeepers, singers) but also of high status as well (priests and descendants of kings) to make the dream work. The lesson here is that no one is excluded from doing the Lord's work. Many people who are in positions of authority tend to forget where they came from, creating a false sense of superiority that they are too good or too great to perform the tasks of those parties beneath them in the chain of command. Do not ever think for a second that you are excluded from the Lord's work because of your status for in God's eyes we all have one status as the body of Christ: his children.

The premise of teamwork is shown repeatedly in the bible to express its effectiveness. The animals boarded the ark two by two. The bible says "...if *two* of you agree here on earth concerning anything you ask, my Father in heaven will do it for you" (Matthew 18:19, New Living Translation). "For where *two* or *three* gather together as my followers, I am there among them" (Matthew 18:20, New Living Translation). Ecclesiastes teaches "A person standing alone can be attacked and defeated, but *two* can stand back-to-back and conquer. *Three* are even better, for a triple-braided cord is not easily broken" (Ecclesiastes 4:12, New Living Translation). And even when we think we are alone just like the man who saw only one set of footprints in the sand (thinking the Lord had abandoned him), we must know that we are not alone for that is when God is with us, carrying us to our dreams, our destiny. Even if teamwork isn't your forte, pledge Team Jesus and the two of you together can make the dream work for that is one team that will never, ever, lose.

Questions:

1. What are the values of teamwork?
2. How can you be a better team player for the body of Christ?

Prayer:

Lord, I realize that I am a part of the body of Christ. Help me to be more receptive to the support of my peers, my co-workers, my friends, my family, but most importantly, to you. Help me to be a support and a team player to those who need me. Give me the vision for the dream so I can assemble my team. In Jesus` name I pray. Amen.

OUT OF THE HEART, THE FACE SPEAKS

Nehemiah 2:2-3

Day 16

Nehemiah 2: 2-3, *New International Version*

- *...so the king asked me, "Why does your face look so sad when you are not ill? This can be nothing but sadness of heart." I was very much afraid, but I said to the king, "May the king live forever! Why should my face not look sad when the city where my ancestors are buried lies in ruins, and its gates have been destroyed by fire?"*

What does your face say about you? I`m not asking about the physical features that make up your facial composition, but more so your mood, your emotions, your expressions. If your face could speak, what would your heart lead it to say, to feel, to be? We live in an age where many choose to wear masks not merely to protect themselves against COVID-19 and other viruses, but to mask our face—an extension of our heart. Some people wear masks to mask the hurt, the pain or even the trauma they carry in their hearts. We use masks as a means to hide our face, so the outside world perceives us as "okay" knowing our heart is metaphorically on fire as life adds more and more fuel to it, seemingly unable to extinguish. A newly-wed`s face might be described as glowing; a young child's face might be described as "bright-eyed and innocent"; a model`s face may be deemed "beat" or stunning. I ask again, what does your face say about you?

During the rule of King Nebuchadnezzar of Babylon (found in the book of 2nd Kings), he conquered Jerusalem, leaving it in ruins, forcing the Jews to live in Babylon as God saw fit to punish them for their disobedience. Years later, some Jews were able to return to Judah (Jerusalem, capital) under the rule of King Artaxerxes of Persia. Nehemiah was a servant of his and upon receiving word that Jerusalem was in ruins and fire burned the city, Nehemiah asked the king to send him to Jerusalem to rebuild the city. Nehemiah approached the king, writing he had never been sad in his presence. The king, reading his face, asked, "Why are you looking so sad? You don't look sick to me. You must be deeply troubled" (Nehemiah 2: 2-3, New International Version). Nehemiah responded, "How can I not be sad? For the city where my ancestors are buried is in ruins, and the gates have been destroyed by fire" (Nehemiah 2:3). In biblical times it was forbidden to be sad in the presence of a king for his presence alone was supposed to make you forget about your problems. (Side thought: If it was forbidden to be sad in the presence of the king, why do we express sadness in the presence of the Lord for he is the source of our joy?) Despite this, Nehemiah did not mask his emotions, but came to the king just as he was for out of his heart, his face spoke.

Even when we take photos for social media, we add these filters to our lives that mask who we are, giving the perception of what we want others to see. Just as the Lord proclaims to come to him as we are, we should present ourselves to the world and others as we truly are, and you will find that that is the doorway to receive the help and support you need. Nehemiah could have approached the king with a "mask" on pretending that everything was all right; but because he was genuine the king granted his wish. I once saw a billboard that said "BeYOUtiful". Being you makes you beautiful. Be you and let the Lord use you for who you are. Let your heart speak for you, for out of the heart, the face speaks.

Questions:
1. What does your face say about you?
2. What do your "masks" say about you?
3. How can you begin to "unmask" to reveal the true you?

Prayer:
Father, help me to be my genuine self. Incline my heart to be filled with Godliness so that my face can speak things only of you. Give me the confidence to "unmask" myself so I can be all of which you have called me to be. In Jesus` name I pray. Amen.

WHAT ONE WOMAN WON'T DO, (GOD WILL)

Esther 1:12

Day 17

Esther 1:12, *Good News Translation*

- *But when the servants told Queen Vashti of the king's command, she refused to come. This made the king furious.*

How would you finish this phrase: what one woman won't do...? Some may answer "I will", "another woman will", "another person will" or even " just won't get done." In our relationships whether they be platonic, intimate, or even short-lived, we each have expectations for each other: communicating good morning and goodnight, comforting each other in times of need, loving unconditionally, or even more specific things like paying the bills, balancing the budget, or even picking the kids up from school. Humans are wired to have these expectations for one another and even ourselves. What tends to put a rift in a relationship is when our expectations exceed reality on a consistent basis. We begin to drift away mentally, then emotionally, physically, and maybe even spiritually. Why? Expectations. Setting expectations and boundaries early in a relationship allows one to know each other, know what is expected, and progress in a more focused, healthy relationship. Although not all of our relationships go in the direction we intend, do know that God does everything for a purpose and although it may feel devastating, heartbreaking, and painful right now, what one woman (or man) won't do, God will.

The book of Esther is a very unique book of the bible. Esther is one book that does not mention the name "God" within it, however God is still on the set. He may not be on the forefront, but he is working behind the scenes. (Side thought: There may be instances in your life where you feel as if God has abandoned you; don't fret, for he is just backstage; God doesn't have to be the star of the show to do his work for he does his best work behind the scenes). As Esther opens, we meet King Xerxes who throws a party for all the men in the kingdom, while his wife, Queen Vashti, throws a separate party for all the ladies in the kingdom. Once King Xerxes got drunk, he sent his servants to fetch Queen Vashti so he could show off her beauty to all in attendance. Scripture writes, "But when the servants told Queen Vashti of the king's command, she refused to come. This made the king furious" (Esther 1:12, Good News Translation). To uphold the reputation of the gender hierarchy and order, the king issued a decree to banish Queen Vashti for her defiance. The king later found a new Queen named Esther, who, with the work of her cousin Mordecai, exposed treachery in the kingdom, saving the life of King Xerxes, protecting his honor while also protecting the Jews against the plots of Haman, a wicked official of Xerxes` court. Logically speaking, if it wasn't for what Queen Vashti didn't do, how would it have allowed for the Lord to do what he does: show up and show out, protecting his own?

In dating, we have all these expectations for our partner; but don't you know the expectation for the Lord exceeds that of *any* human? What human can walk on water? What human can make a meal fit for five, serve 5,000? What human can raise the dead? What one woman won't do, God will. The bible states in Ephesians 3:20, "Now unto him that is able to do exceeding abundantly above all that we ask or think…" (King James Version). Paul is telling us that whatever we ask or think, God will do above that to give us abundance, then exceed that abundance. What human on earth can fulfill this promise other than a God who can do all things but fail? FILL IN THE BLANK: What one _____ won't do, God will!

Questions:
1. What expectations do you have for yourself to grow closer to Christ?
2. What expectations do you have for your relationship to help you both grow closer to Christ?
3. What expectations do you have for the Lord to do in your life this week? Month? Year? Lifetime?

Prayer:
Father, thank you for exceeding expectations. Help me to realize that the ups and downs in my natural relationships and even spiritual relationship with you are for a purpose, and that I must look to you for the fruits of expectation that no man or woman on earth can fulfill. I'm expecting bigger, better, and greater! Thanking you in advance, in Jesus` name I pray. Amen.

DOUBLE FOR YOUR TROUBLE

Job 42:10

Day 18

Job 42:10, *New International Version*

- *After Job had prayed for his friends, the Lord restored his fortunes and gave him twice as much as he had before.*

What is one thing that is easy to get into, but hard to get out of? Trouble: something we can't seem to escape. In relationships, when the male is in trouble, he gets sent to the "doghouse." When children get in trouble at school, they get sent to the principal's office, get detention, or serve out-of-school or in-school suspension. When we get in trouble with the law, we get some sort of consequence or serve jail time. When we don`t pay or report taxes accurately, we get in trouble with the government and IRS. Did you know you were born into trouble? Job 5:7 declares, "Yet man is born to trouble as surely as sparks fly upward" (New International Version). But, the bible assures us, "In this world you will have trouble. But take heart! I have overcome the world" (John 16:33, New International Version). Jesus is telling us he has worn every trouble this world dishes to us; in other words, he overcame our every trouble. Sit back, relax, and expect double for your trouble!

Many of Christians are familiar with the story of Job. Satan decides to put Job to the test of his faith, thinking that Job would curse God when dealt pain and suffering; God assures Satan that Job would not turn his back on the Lord despite any test the Devil assigns. In one day, 24 hours, 86,400 seconds, Job receives word that his livestock has died, servants have died, and ten children have died—all from varying circumstances. In addition, Job became afflicted with skin sores, causing his wife to urge him to "Curse God and die" (Job 2:9, New Living Translation). During Job`s tests and trials, he begins to question God—not directly, however; but he still manages to not succumb to the devil's schemes despite the ill-advised advice given to him from his friends. In the last chapter of the book of Job, God "texts back" and gives Job a series of rhetorical questions, teaching Job his ignorance to God's power. Job repented. Although God was angry with Job's friends for offering Job such misguided information about God, the bible declares, "After Job had prayed for his friends, the Lord restored his fortunes and gave him twice as much as he had before" (Job 42: 10, New International Version). Notice Job did not pray for himself or his circumstance, but despite all he had against him, he prayed for his friends. Job interceded on behalf of sinners, earnestly praying for them. God saw fit to reward Job with double for his trouble, granting him renewed health, long life, more property than he had previously, and new children.

In life, we all ask these questions: Why do the good suffer while the wicked prosper? God, do you hear me? How can I believe in you if I`ve never seen you? How can a good God exist amongst an evil world? What is even more troubling is when we ask these questions amongst financial hardship, amongst health complications, amongst depression and anxiety, amongst out-of-control youth, amongst death and disease, amongst backstabbers and liars, amongst corruption and evil, amongst fear and famine, and even amongst spiritual attacks. The list of sin and evil is never-ending, yet we serve a God who can grant double for our trouble. What I like about this Scripture is that because Job was selfless, praying for others and not himself in a time of trouble, God blessed him with double. Despite your struggles, pray a selfless prayer for others and watch God give you *and* those you intercede on, double for both your trouble.

Questions:

1. What in life is troubling you?
2. What types of questions do you ask God or would you ask God? Why?
3. Do you pray more for yourself or others?
4. What steps can you take to pray more selflessly than selfishly?

Prayer:

Father: Help me to pray more selflessly. God, you know my circumstances and you know my struggles, but God you declare in your word that "Greater is he that is in me, than he that is in the world." The world needs prayer for they lack the power I have within me. I pray for my neighborhood, my city, my state, my country, my world. Heal this land from all sin that tempts us daily. In Jesus` name I pray. Amen.

ANOTHER DAY WITH HIS BENEFITS

Psalms 103:2

Day 19

Psalm 103:2, *English Standard Version*

- *Bless the Lord, O my soul, and forget not all his benefits:*

When searching for a new career, there are often three main determinants we use to place us in the most ideal workplace; one of these determinants is location. With the growing prices of fuel in our current economy, so many people seek careers that they can bike to, walk to, or even work remotely. The second determining factor we use to find the ideal workplace is pay. Having a history in retail, this economy does nothing but grant me anxiety, seeing a 12 case of soda raise from $3.99 to $7.99 in a matter of months, to see products getting smaller yet the price stay the same, and to even notice how what we call "on sale", merely be what the regular price was. The last, yet not least important factor we consider in the job search is the benefits: COVID pay, profitable retirement plan, doctor/dental insurance, overtime/holiday/weekend hours and offerings, drivetime compensation, vacation and sick time accrual, disability, and even employee discounts. Despite all these benefits, how many of you know that the benefits of another *day* with Jesus outweigh any *annual* benefits a job or career can offer?

It is in the book of Psalms that we learn of David: his life, his rule (though threatened by many) and his victories (unifying Israel under one rule). David is marked with obedience, selflessness, and leadership in his roles as a shepherd, musician, warrior, and king. In this psalm, David begins to recall the blessings of the Lord as he reaches the latter part of his life as he is overcome with praise for Him. Three times, in the first two verses, David calls upon himself to render praises to the Lord. He continues, "Bless the Lord, O my soul, and forget not all his benefits" (Psalms 103:2, English Standard Version). David proceeds to tell us of just some of the benefits, writing: "He forgives all my sins and heals all my diseases; he redeems me from death and crowns me with love and tender mercies; he fills my life with good things; he gives righteousness and justice to all who are treated unfairly; his anger is only for a moment; he does not punish us for all our sins, but has removed all our sins; he does not deal harshly with us, as we deserve" (Psalms 103, New Living Translation). It is easy for us to proclaim we've had a bad day if we only judge what we see in the natural realm but look at the benefits the Lord provides us for one day in the spiritual realm. The many good spiritual benefits he provides outweigh any bad day in the natural scheme of things.

On our Christian walk we often get caught up in the motion of life that we sometimes forget the gift that keeps on giving. Given any typical job or career, the benefit package is often different for a part time employee compared to a full-time employee or even different for a manager than it is for a worker at a lower level. But what is so special about the benefit package that God offers is that it does not vary whether you are for him or against him, whether you claim him or don't claim him, whether you know him or don`t know him; whether you are rich or poor; black or white; housed or homeless; gay or straight; a pastor or a member; or even well-educated or uneducated; his benefit package remains the same for we all have one title in heaven: servant. One might think that this Christian work is not a job, but Merriam-Webster dictionary defines the word "job" as "a task or piece of work, especially one that is paid." So, if we are receiving payment from God through his benefits, this Christian work is *our* job and God does not want us to reap the benefits for fruitless labor. He wants us to work, bringing glory to his name, making disciples of all nations. Continue to do his work, follow his will, and he will provide a way for your benefits to fall fresh from heaven and overflow into our lives, our ministry, and ultimately, to our world.

Questions:

1. Are you satisfied with your spiritual paycheck this week despite the number of hours you put in for the Lord?
2. What are some other benefits besides the ones from Psalms 103 that the Lord provides?

Prayer:

Father: I thank you for your benefits that you provide me even when I don't put in the necessary time with you. I thank you for your grace and your mercy for paying me even when I take sick days, vacation days, holidays, and personal leave from you, when you never leave nor forsake me. Thank you for your benefits and help me to work for you and your kingdom each and every day. In Jesus` name I pray. Amen.

MISSED CALL AND ONE NEW VOICEMAIL

Proverbs 8:1

Day 20

Proverbs 8:1, *English Standard Version*

- *Does not wisdom call? Does not understanding raise her voice?*

Here's a riddle. Despite the series of statements, there is only **one** answer. I call but some refuse to answer. I am always right. I am better than silver and gold. I live with good judgment, common sense, and success. If you love me, I`ll love you; if you love me, you`ll inherit wealth. I have riches and honor as well as wealth and justice. I walk in righteousness. I was formed before creation and will exist long after. If you find me, I can give you life and favor from the Lord. You can use me to solve this riddle. What am I?

In the 21st century, telemarketers have reached an all-time high with their use of spam calls. Ranging from stolen social security numbers to a nephew in a county jail to requests inquiring about your car's extended warranty, we get tired of answering the phone to these schemes. While mobile carriers try their best to restrict these calls to our devices, a few still manage to get through to us. I don`t believe I am the only one with this issue, but sometimes when declining spam calls, the automated spam system leaves a voicemail, usually consisting of the spam telemarketer voice assistant rambling on and on. This causes us to have to check our voicemails often to rid the voicemail of unwanted messages. This process of ridding our devices of spam calls and messages angers many individuals while also disrupting our daily lives. On the contrary, we do often receive calls and voicemails that are important, vital, and necessary. These calls and voicemails serve a purpose to our lives and often come in handy when we do miss important calls. While these electronic processes are integral, there is one call that will not come directly to our landline, cellphone, pager, beeper, watch, or any other device with cellular connectivity. This call I am speaking about is from wisdom; but there is good news, if you miss the call, wisdom will leave you a voicemail.

Solomon is credited as the author of the book of Proverbs, the wise king who asked God for wisdom and discernment. Proverbs 1 details the purpose of the book: "...to teach people wisdom and discipline, to help them understand the insights of the wise. Their purpose is to teach people to live disciplined and successful lives, to help them do what is right, just, and fair" (Proverbs 1:2-3, New Living Translation). The book of Proverbs offers wisdom and insight on trust, parenting, and immoral women (considering Solomon is the writer), with the final chapters offering specific proverbs from Agur and King Lemuel. In Proverbs 8:1, Solomon writes, "Does not wisdom call? Does not understanding raise her voice?" (Proverbs 8:1, English Standard Version). Solomon is teaching us that wisdom doesn't call everyone, and it is wrongful for us to assume that (just as it is wrongful to assume everyone has common sense), but even though wisdom doesn't *call* everyone, she does, however, raise her voice; it is up to us to listen. In other words, even if you miss the call, wisdom leaves a voicemail loud enough for you to hear, if only you find the time and possess the open-mindedness to listen and accept it as a means to grow wiser.

It is often said, "knowledge" is acquired in books and "wisdom" is gained from life and experiences. If the bible is the Book of Life, it is one pathway to wisdom. Because wisdom is gained through experience, I wondered how I, at 24 years of age, can receive wisdom when I have not lived enough to learn enough. I thought about how Solomon gained wisdom despite only being in his twenties when he became king. Solomon—younger than I am with *more* responsibility. God showed me that Solomon asked God for it, and he received it. Yes, wisdom may be gained from reading the bible of the most-wise king; wisdom is gained from living and learning from mistakes; but the bible says in James 1:5, "If you need wisdom, ask our generous God, and he will give it to you. He will not rebuke you for asking" (New Living Translation). Ask God for wisdom, and as you live, you`ll learn. As you live, you`ll begin to possess a thing better than silver and gold; as you live you'll begin to live with good judgment, common sense, and success; as you live you`ll love wisdom and wisdom will love you; as you live you`ll inherit riches, honor, wealth, justice, righteousness, life and favor. No longer will the riddle be who am I and the answer be wisdom; the riddle will be who am I and the answer will be you. Walk in your wisdom!

Questions:

1. What does wisdom look like to you? What does having wisdom feel like to you? What does having wisdom sound like to you?
2. Why do you want God to grant you wisdom?
3. How can you walk into and in wisdom?

Prayer:

Father: Allow me to not miss my appointment with wisdom. Give me revelation, insight, and discernment so that I can receive the wisdom you so graciously give. Open my heart and mind to receive your wisdom each and every day. Speak to me. Guide me. Direct me. In Jesus` name I pray. Amen.

WHAT TIME IS IT?

Ecclesiastes 3:1

Day 21

Ecclesiastes 3:1, *God's Word Translation*

- *Everything has its own time, and there is a specific time for every activity under heaven:*

In the Marvel Studio`s series *Loki*, Loki and his companion Sylvie are on a quest to apprehend a variant (being) who kills TVA agents. The TVA is the Time Variance Authority and their job is to prevent people from diverging from the Sacred Timeline. Essentially, the TVA has a life path for all humans and when they diverge from it they create a Nexus Event, the formation of a new timeline branching from the Sacred Timeline. In charge of the Sacred Timeline are the Timekeepers, three unknown beings. Loki and Sylvie try to find the time-keepers so they can be released from the captivity of the TVA, in hopes of finding these time-keepers to convince them to put them back on the Sacred Timeline. In their quest, they finally manage to find the time-keepers, unintentionally beheading one of them, realizing they are "fake, mindless androids" that do not control time at all and that there must be a more supreme being in charge of time. In reality, time is a man-made concept and we as humans believe that our "mindless androids" and apple devices dictate time. We are under false assumptions that clocks tell us when to leave for work or when to arrive at appointments. We set alarms and think they wake us up in the morning. I ask you, what time is it?

The author of Ecclesiastes is a "wise man", opening the book, "everything is meaningless, completely meaningless" (Ecclesiastes 1:1, New Living Translation), adopting a more nihilistic philosophy. He continues, "The greater my wisdom, the greater my grief" (Ecclesiastes 1: 18, New Living Translation). The wise man decides that since wisdom wasn`t working, he'd try pleasure in drinking, acquiring property and vineyards, owning flocks, collecting silver and gold, and even by sexual gratification of women, still feeling empty inside—meaningless. Despite this realization, the last chapter of the book is more hopeful, as the writer urges us to remember God in everything because life is a cycle and we all inevitably will return to God when life is over. I ask you again, what time is it? After complaining for 12 1/2 chapters about the pessimistic nature of life, the writer offers a subtle glimpse of optimism, similar to the binary oppositions (concepts opposite in meaning) offered in Ecclesiastes 3: While there may be a time to die, there is a time to be born; while there may be a time to kill, there is a time to heal; while there may be a time to tear down, there is a time to build up;

while there may be a time to grieve, there is a time to dance; while there may be a time to hate, there is a time to love; while there may be a time for war, there is also a time for peace" (Ecclesiastes 3, New Living Translation). The "wise man" is teaching us nothing which we are not familiar with. We know life has its highs and lows, hills and valleys; but the wise man is teaching us that time may be filled with swift transition, but God is our timekeeper, and his timing is perfect.

What time is it in your life? I`m not asking for the man-made clock time, I`m asking if God has you on mountain time or valley time, high time or low time, a good time or a bad time. What time zone are you in? The peace time zone or the war; the killing time zone or the healing; the weeping time zone or the laughing? What does your clock read: planting or uprooting, tearing or building; mourning or dancing. No matter our relationship to Christ, we are all susceptible to trials and tribulations, but we must realize that no matter the timestamp on our life, God is our timekeeper. Don`t worry because he has you for this "time" shall pass and God`s reception is so perfect that he can be reached no matter if your clock is stuck on valley time or if it is ticking on mountain time. What time is it in your life?

Questions:
1. How would you best describe the "time" in your life right now?
2. How can you remain encouraged despite the "time zone" you may currently be in?

Prayer:
Father: I thank you for your time. Your timing is perfect, and you orchestrate time so well that I will put all my trust in your timing. Help me to lift you up when I`m on "valley time" and help me to bow down to you when I`m on "mountain time". I thank you that no matter the "time zone" I`m in, you`re still right there with me. Allow me to always feel your presence. In Jesus` name I pray. Amen.

WHAT'S LOVE GOT TO DO WITH IT?

Song of Solomon 8:6

Day 22

Song of Solomon 8:6, *New Living Translation*

- *For love is as strong as death...*

In the year 1984, Tina Turner recorded one of her most popular songs called "What's Love Got to Do with It?" Turner had hesitancy in producing the song, but her manager convinced her otherwise. The song explores a relationship between a woman and a man, but the woman feels no emotional attachment to the man. She wrote the song letting her partner know that their relationship is merely physical, with no love connection. How many of you have had these encounters of sexual intimacy with no love connection, seeking merely to indulge, entertain, or satisfy fleeting, carnal, sexual pleasures? I am speaking about the "friends with benefits" package, the "one-night stands", the "hit em and quit em" encounters, the booty calls, or even situationships. Near the end of the song Turner asks, "What`s love but a sweet old-fashioned notion?" implying that while the encounter may have been sweet, love is merely uncommon, antiquated, or out-of-style. Seemingly, living in a loveless world with murder, trafficking, suicide, war, and conflict at an all-time high, there is still a man who loves us unconditionally, unequivocally, and unbiasedly. God's love is not man's love and God's love has *everything* to do with who we are and whose we are.

Song of Solomon is a book of love shared between a man and a woman. The book is a poem of the two expressing their love for each other in a tender-hearted tone. In the last chapter of the book, Solomon states, "Place me like a seal over your heart, like a seal on your arm" (Song of Solomon 8:6, New Living Translation). If we think about a seal, its purpose is twofold: to hold things in and to block things out. Solomon wants the woman to not only contain his love for him in her heart, but he also wants her to block out love (romantic love) from other men. He continues, "For love is as strong as death..." (Song of Solomon 8:6, New Living Translation). Using the seal analogy, if you have an open wound with no seal on it, you are susceptible to disease and infection. If you have an open heart, metaphorically, you are susceptible to being infected by multiple lovers, using and abusing you each time, making it hard for you to love and trust as your heart—metaphorically—begins to die as you lose parts of yourself with each "love infection", not "love connection."

While this book is based on love between men and women, I choose to view it through the lens of Godly love, for his love is never-ending. His love cannot infect you. His love cannot hurt you. His love cannot damage you. His love cannot leave you. His love cannot end with you. The bible teaches, "We love because he first loved us" (1 John 4:19, English Standard Version). Tina Turner asked the question, "What's love got to do with it?" Love has everything to do with it. We live because he loves. Solomon was wrong too, for he writes, "Love is as strong as death" (Song of Solomon 8:6, New Living Translation). Love is stronger than death for love was nailed to a cross, love was buried in a tomb, and love rose three days later with all power in his hands. Love is stronger than death for love lifted us. Love is stronger than death for love completes us. Love is stronger than death for love loved us before we loved ourselves. Don't rely on the love of humanity for that love will one day fade; rely on the "overwhelming, never-ending, reckless" love of God. His love has *everything* to do with it.

Questions:

1. What is love?
2. How would you describe God's love?
3. How do you know God loves you?
4. What are markers of Godly love (he to you; you to others; you to self)?

Prayer:

Father: I love you. Thank you for loving me even when I don`t love myself. Thank you for loving me even when I don't always show and express love to you. Thank you for sending your son Jesus to die so that I have a chance to live, love, and be loved by you. I love you and thank you. In Jesus` name I pray. Amen.

OLD NEWS

Isaiah 43:18

Day 23

Isaiah 43:18, *English Standard Version*

- *"Remember not the former things, nor consider the things of old. Behold, I am doing a new thing; now it springs forth, do you not perceive it?*

My family (me, being the exception) are Dallas Cowboy fans. If you`re not a fan, do keep reading, revelation loading. When it is time for them to play, they make a big deal about it and glue themselves to a comfortable seat to watch every possession, play, and period. My aunt got home from church one evening and turned the television on. Upon seeing that the Cowboys were playing, she wondered why my uncle (an even bigger fan of the Cowboys) did not tell her they were playing today, let alone he not be there for them both to watch and enjoy. She told me afterwards that as she sat there, she could feel her blood pressure rising due to the anxiety of the Cowboys possibly making the playoffs. As the game came to a conclusion, my Uncle had returned home and she asked him about the game. He stood there perplexed, later explaining the Cowboys did not play that afternoon, leaving my aunt in a state of perplexity. My uncle then told her that the game she was watching was a rerun of an earlier game. I found revelation in this as she was getting all worked up, anxious, and stressed over old news that had already passed. How often do we fret over old news when God is ready to do new things in our lives? How often do we reminisce on our past and unearth old anxieties, old circumstances, old friends, old situations, old news?

Isaiah, a renowned biblical prophet, wrote an account of the sin of the Israelites as they continually disobeyed God on their trek to the Promised Land. While the book asserts a heavy and dejected tone for the Israelites, Isaiah does prophecy the coming of the Messiah who will judge not only them, but humanity. Isaiah uses a series of "he was" statements, writing, "He was despised and rejected; he was pierced for our rebellion; he was beaten so we could be whole; he was whipped so we could be healed; he was oppressed and treated harshly; he was led like a lamb to the slaughter; he was led away; he was struck down for the rebellion of my people; he was buried like a criminal; he was put in a rich man's grave; he was counted among and he bore the sins of many and interceded for rebels" (Isaiah 53, New Living Translation). Declare today that "he was, therefore, I am!"

The reason I chose to highlight Isaiah 53 before expounding on Isaiah 43 is because I want you to understand the "new news" before backtracking into the "old news." The old news of sin is nothing compared to the new news of the Savior. The old news of death is nothing compared to the new news of dominion. The old news of rejection is nothing compared to our newfound relationship with Christ. His piercing has no comparison to his power. His whipping has no comparison to his wonder. His oppression has no comparison to our opportunities with him. Stop sinking and soaking in your sin for Jesus died so we can live. I`m not saying to disregard your past or where you`ve come from, but to begin to thank God for this new life we have in him. Isaiah prophesied, "I am doing a new thing; do you not perceive it?" (Isaiah 43:18, English Standard Version). How can we see the new thing if our attention and focus is on things of the past—old news? Have hope in your future for our Savior is doing a new thing in you, through you, and with you; you just have to keep your eyes on new news and stop changing the channel to watch the old news.

Questions:

1. What "old news" exists in your life (events, people, attitudes, perspectives etc)?
2. Why are you thankful for the newness of life that Jesus` death and resurrection allowed?
3. What "new things" are you expecting God to do for you? How can you continually perceive and believe in it?

Prayer:

Father: I thank you for old news: old news of you and old news of me. I realize that old news allows me to walk into my "new thing." Allow me not to make yearly resolutions, but daily devotions to you so that I can have a fresh and new anointing, purpose, passion, and a sense of power each day. In Jesus` name I pray. Amen.

GIANTS FALL

Jeremiah 50:2

Day 24

Jeremiah 50:2, *New Living Translation*

- *"...tell everyone that Babylon will fall!"*

Andrew Carnegie. John D. Rockefeller. J.P. Morgan. Cornelius Vanderbilt. Henry Ford. These men are dubbed the "men who built America", each for their contributions as monopolistic enterprises that transformed and revolutionized America for the better. As their monopolies began to grow, America started to realize the dominance, power, status, prestige, wealth, and influence they had on the American economy. Signed and approved into U.S law on July 2, 1890, the Sherman Anti-trust Act was the first of a few acts or laws that outlawed monopolistic business practices as the American government tried to restore order in stabilizing the American economy. These monopolies would become so powerful that they drove out competition and this act sought to restore competition in American society. Thirteen years later, anti-monopolist Lizzie Maggie created the first Monopoly-like game to illustrate and educate individuals on the negative, monopolistic practices and aspects from which these men operated. If you have ever played the popular game, you don't simply play to play, you play to win or to dominate. You play to establish as much property, wealth, status, and influence to own "streets", adding houses and hotels to build your empire. Typically, when players reach this level of success owning multiple streets and houses and hotels, players get arrogant, snobby—prideful. Although this pride exists in a fictional sense, it is that same attitude in life that allows us to be our own enemy, cause our own demise, and bring about our own destruction.

The book of Jeremiah is said to have been written in conjunction with the Israelite prophet Jeremiah and his scribe Baruch. Jeremiah was called to warn Israel of breaking their covenant with God as they continually pledged allegiance to gods and not God, leading to Jerusalem`s downfall. Way before the Carnegie`s, Rockefeller`s, Morgan`s, Vanderbilt`s and Ford`s of the world was the very first monopoly: Babylon. Viewed as a biblical symbol of power and might, Babylon`s monopoly can be traced to the book of Genesis. Genesis 11 details the migration of people to Babylon, saying, "Let's build a great city for ourselves with a tower that reaches into the sky. This will make us famous..." (New Living Translation). God saw this prideful, united act and decided to confuse the people, causing the people to speak many different languages so they could not understand each other, scattering them all over the world. Fast forwarding 23 books later, Babylon finally built their monopoly. As Jeremiah urged the Israelites to turn back to God to no avail, God allowed King Nebuchadnezzar and the country of Babylon to seize and destroy Jerusalem to punish the Israelites' disobedience to God. At this point, I can imagine the people of Babylon feeling the utmost pride and superiority as God used them to punish the nation of Israel. But Babylon—the same nation used by God to punish Israel—also got punished. Jeremiah prophesied, "...tell everyone that Babylon will fall" (Jeremiah 50:2, New Living Translation).

You thought the message of this devotional was the typical "giants fall" cliché about the giants or problems in our life falling prey to us; but the message in this devotion is that sometimes we become our own giants. We grow so high and mighty that we think we cannot be defeated. Notice the same nation used to punish Israel, later God punishes. We all answer to one God: his name is Jesus. The Babylonians never saw destruction coming because they were blinded by their pride. In our lives we give ourselves too much credit that we begin to think that we are a solo act with no stage crew. As God grants us favor and increase for our talents and gifts, we become prideful, representing that monopoly mentality of being large and in-charge. Do not become so consumed in what you think you`ve earned, because you've accomplished nothing. Reflect on you, your pride. Don't become a victim of your own destruction and demise. Do not be a giant, for soon, you too will fall. Put your pride aside. Do not fall.

Questions:
1. What talents and gifts do you possess—aspects or qualities in which you excel?
2. When have you exhibited pride in your talents and/or gifts? Did you "fall?" How did it feel?
3. How can you be less prideful and more purposeful in giving God the credit for your talents and gifts?

Prayer:
Father: I thank you for your grace for when I had my "giant" mentality and had given myself the credit for my success, your grace is what covered me. I thank you for your gifts and talents for which you provide me. Help me to use them for your glory so I can walk into my purpose—not with pride, but giving you all the praise. In Jesus` name I pray. Amen.

GET COMFORTABLE

Lamentations 1:16

Day 25

Lamentations 1:16, *New Living Translation*

- *"For all these things I weep; tears flow down my cheeks. No one is here to comfort me; any who might encourage me are far away.*

On Friday, May 6, 2022, God saw fit to take my mother home to her heavenly palace. Leading up to her new life, a common theme that ran through the speech of the doctors was the idea of comfort. Many of them would argue, "We just want her to be comfortable" or "her comfort is the most important thing right now". Doctors administer different medicines for seemingly end-of-life patients, but how many of you know that God is the only necessary medicine needed for comfort? Whether the doctors and nurses define comfort as physically comfortable or in preparation for someone's passing, the kind of comfort that God provides is spiritual. The kind of comfort that God provides is the kind that can take a loved one from you but shower you with peace that surpasses all understanding. The kind of comfort God provides is the kind where you can have no money in the bank but have no worry in your heart. The kind of comfort that God provides is the kind that the doctor may tell you all hope is lost, but makes you reply, "my hope is here." The kind of comfort that God provides is the kind that makes you not worry about what tomorrow holds because you already know who holds tomorrow. The kind of comfort that God provides is the kind that allows you to walk on the car lot with no money, no credit, and no cosigner, but allows you to leave with what you came for. Get comfortable.

The book of Lamentations is written by an anonymous author who witnessed the siege (destruction and exile) of Jerusalem. Further, the author uses a poetic structure to lament (express sorrow, regret, or grief) and/or memorialize individuals who died during the fall of Jerusalem. The poet uses this space to vent emotions, personifying Jerusalem and its inhabitants, describing them as: "mournful, having nowhere to turn, full of grief and despair, captured, starving, weak, broken, humiliated, defiled, despised, devastated, helpless, punished, trampled, and without comfort" (Lamentations 1). How often do we describe our lives or our situations as one or even a combination of these words? Get comfortable in being uncomfortable but take comfort in God for people cannot comfort us nor do people have the power to change or truly empathize with us. Isaiah 66:13 reminds us, "As a mother comforts her child, so will I [God] comfort you" (New International Version). God wants to comfort us in the manner of a mother comforting her own. Why do we turn to earthly treasures and pleasures when God is simply asking us, "Can I hold you too close *for* comfort?" He wants to hold us so we are comforted. Ask God to wrap you in his loving arms for every time you face a crisis, God says you are one step closer to comfort. God is never too close for comfort, nor too far away in your crisis. When troubles rise, don`t think of them as a stumbling block, but a means for God to comfort you even more. Get comfortable.

There was a survey conducted amongst Americans to identify the top 30 things that provide Americans comfort. The top contenders on the list included stretching, meditating, taking a hot shower or bath, wearing thick blankets and socks, getting a massage, going for a brisk walk in nature, coloring, or even journaling or reading. While these are all things that may bring comfort to our lives, I propose that we add to the top of the list: having a genuine relationship with the Lord. God can provide you more comfort than that Lazyboy recliner, than that Sleep Number bed, than that Serta mattress, than that 30-way power adjustable driver seat, than that first-class airplane ticket, than that Sherpa blanket, than that Skechers house shoe, than those Bamboo sheets, than that Tempur-Pedic pillow, *and* that first stretch of the morning combined. For he is all the comfort that you need, so get comfortable! Don`t think of your grief and distress as punishment but think of it as being one step closer to comfort. Get comfortable.

Questions:

1. What is your level of comfort in and with life right now: very uncomfortable, uncomfortable, neutral, comfortable, very comfortable? Why?
2. Are you comfortable physically? Socially? Emotionally? Spiritually? Financially?
3. How can you become more comfortable despite life's circumstances?

Prayer:

Father: Thank you for the comfort you show me each day. Thank you for shifting my mindset in that when distress is here, you hold me closer to comfort; when trials arise, you hold me closer to comfort; when life happens, you hold me closer to comfort. Hold me close. Help me become comfortable with you despite the discomforts of life. In Jesus` name I pray. Amen.

TOUGH SKIN

Ezekiel 3:8

Day 26

Ezekiel 3: 8, *Good News Translation*

- *Now I will make you as stubborn and as tough as they are.*

The truth hurts. As time marches on, people have become increasingly vocal in voicing truth. When the term *"sugarcoat"* became a word during the 1870`s, it originally meant "coat with sugar." People would often coat their medicine with sugar to make it more appealing or palatable. My mother once told me that when she was in school, they would often receive sugar cubes, but she did not know why at the time. As she lived, she learned that they were administered sugar cubes with the polio vaccine in order to make it more appealing for kids to digest since the vaccine—invented by a man named Albert Sabin—had a bitter, salty taste. Similarly, the popular Mary Poppin`s song called "A Spoonful of Sugar" derived from Sabin`s five year-old son who had explained to him that he swallowed the polio vaccine with some sugar to mask the unappetizing taste of it. During the 1900`s, the term *"sugarcoat"* took a more figurative meaning, defined as expressing the truth in a less offensive, but more pleasant manner to prevent hurting someone's feelings—making it more appealing to the receiver. As we live and learn in a desensitized world, it seems as if more and more people choose not to sugarcoat anything, possibly due to media (news, social media, television etc.) portrayals offering constant reminders that reveal the hard truths of life. Because of this shift in reality, it is challenging to exist in this world without having tough skin: possessing the ability to take criticism, to accept hard truths about ourselves given to us by others, and even to "keep it 100" or "real" with others at all times.

The prophet and priest, Ezekiel, lived in Jerusalem during the first Babylon attack, in which Babylon spared Jerusalem. Ezekiel was one of the members led into exile and subject to Babylonian captivity. The book of Ezekiel begins five years later as Ezekiel turns 30 years of age. Similar to the task of Jeremiah, God tasked Ezekiel with urging the Israelites to obey God; on the contrary if they did not, they would be subject to destruction (inevitably happening). Time and time again, God sends the Israelites messengers to warn them of their actions, yet they do not receive the hard truths Ezekiel relayed from God. God, knowing the fate of the Israelites, warned Ezekiel early in the book that "...the people of Israel won't listen to you any more than they listen to me! For the whole lot of them are hard-hearted and stubborn" (Ezekiel 3:7, New Living Translation). From their hard hearts, derives the message of this devotional: tough skin. In an attempt to not fully discourage Ezekiel of "relaying his

[God`s] messages", God said, "I will make you...as tough as they are" (Ezekiel 3:8). God is saying in spite of the Israelites stubborn, disobedient, and inattentive nature, he is going to give Ezekiel tough skin to deliver his messages to the Israelites—not in the manner of sugarcoating anything, but by relaying the hard truth verbatim as God gave those messages to Ezekiel.

If God gives you a message or the urge to tell somebody the hard truth, tell them, for it is your responsibility. God told Ezekiel if you don't relay my messages as given, the sin of Israel would become his (Ezekiel`s) responsibility. Many people are not gifted with the ability to tell someone the hard truth without sugarcoating it, but if God lays it on your heart or instructs you to "keep it real" with a friend, a family member, a co-worker, a church member, or any other individual, you have to obey him or you become the victim of disobedience. You have to wear the tough skin necessary to relay the message no matter how the other individual receives or reacts to it. There may be a falling out, a backlash, a sore spot, or even a break-up for relaying the message; but if God urges you to tell them, it is for the best and not the worst. Some apples have tough skin, and it may be hard to swallow, but do you know that the tough skin of the apple is where the most nutrients and vitamins are found? Yes, it may be hard to chew, swallow, and digest, but you have bettered yourself. The truth is no different. Truth hurts, but when you are able to chew (receive) and swallow (accept) the tough skin of truth, you have bettered yourself. It may hurt in the moment to digest it, but that tough skin of truth will benefit you eventually. That tough skin may be the wisdom God needs you to give *or* receive in that season of your life to take yours or another individual's life to a new level.

Questions:
1. How can you exhibit tough skin in giving or receiving hard truths?
2. How easy is it for you to tell someone hard truths about them or their situation?
3. Have you ever had to give someone a "tough skin" lesson? How did it affect you? How did it affect the other individual?
4. What benefits lie in having "tough skin"?

Prayer:
Father: I submit to your obedience. I realize that the truth hurts, but I pray that you give me the tough skin necessary to *impart* Godly wisdom, guidance, and hard truths to others. I pray that you give me the tough skin necessary to *receive* Godly wisdom, guidance, and hard truths. Help me to realize the truth may be hard to give and to digest, but I declare and decree any message you have for me is for the betterment of me and my life. Thank you for tough skin. In Jesus` name I pray. Amen.

QUALIFIED, BUT NOT CHOSEN

Daniel 1:18-19

Day 27

Daniel 1: 18-19, *New Living Translation*

- *When the training period ordered by the king was completed, the chief of staff brought all the young men to King Nebuchadnezzar. The king talked with them, and no one impressed him as much as Daniel, Hananiah, Mishael, and Azariah. So they entered the royal service.*

Every single job or career on the planet has standards set in place for each position. Before we begin to apply for jobs, we all look at the job requirements to see how close our skill set and qualifications match the requirements the job expects. After applying for the position, the next step is the interview process. Typically, after an interview, employers will tell you one of four things: "You're hired", "We`re strongly considering you...", "We may have hired you, but..." or "We'll be in touch." "You're hired" is self-explanatory. "We`re strongly considering you" is a way of stating you fit here, but so do some other people who interviewed, therefore, once we review all of the applications and interviews side-by-side, we`ll pick the best individual for the position. "We may have hired you, but..." is a way of stating one: that you and I both know we can't hire you with this "red flag" on your record; but good shot, or two: there is something from your resume, your interview, or your past that your employer does not want to chance in hiring you. "We'll be in touch" can either be completely positive or completely negative: either they know they'll hire you but don't want to tell you yet to mask desperation or eagerness, or they know they have no chance of hiring you and hope you don't call them, but *if* you do, they`ll just give you the runaround. Despite the outcome, what bothers us the most is that when we know we have a stellar resume, no red flags on our background check, great prior recommendations from previous employers, several years of experience to do the job well, and even meet and/or exceed the qualifications. What bothers us the most is when we know we`re qualified, but not chosen.

After the first Babylonian attack (led by King Nebuchadnezzar) on Jerusalem, existed four Israelites from the royal family of David: Daniel, Hananiah, Mishael, Azariah (more commonly known as Shadrach, Meshach, Abednego). King Nebuchadnezzar sent for his chief of staff Ashpenaz to bring him some of the Babylonian captives. Nebuchadnezzar did not want any ordinary men but had certain job requirements. The men had to be "strong, healthy, good-looking, well-versed in every branch of learning, gifted with knowledge and good judgment, and suited to serve" (Daniel 1:4, New Living Translation). Once selected, the "potential employees" needed to conduct three years of on-the-job training to learn the language and literature of Babylon to enter the royal service. Daniel and his three friends were chosen. Daniel refused to eat the food and drink the wine of the king (since it may have been a product of an idolatrous sacrifice) and was able to influence Ashpenaz to allow him and his friends to only eat a diet consisting of vegetables and water. After ten days, the bible writes, "Daniel and his three friends looked healthier and better nourished than the young men who had been eating the food assigned by the king" (Daniel 1: 15, New Living Translation). When the three years of on-the-job-training was complete, Ashpenaz brought *all* the young men (Daniel, his three friends, and the other recruits not mentioned) to the king. No one impressed King Nebuchadnezzar as much as Daniel and his three friends, so they were chosen to enter the royal service. All the young men were qualified, yet only four were chosen.

When King Nebuchadnezzar posted the position, he posted it with only six job requirements, but after the on-the job training, Daniel was overqualified as he gained integrity in not eating the king's food showing his faithfulness to God *and* God have him the ability to interpret meanings of dreams and visions. My message here is that while life is so large, one large aspect of life is our jobs and careers. We depend on them to make a living, and it can almost become a dogfight seeing people who get hired after you make more than you *and* you end up training them or you being qualified for a promotion, yet you weren't the one chosen. I want you to know that that job, that career, that opportunity, that open door, that position, that responsibility, that raise, that promotion is out there for you. I can imagine how the young men in the book of Daniel felt after training for three years, just to be told you're qualified, but are not chosen. As you go through life you may qualify for the job, the loan, Medicare and Medicaid, unemployment, a rebate, and even government assistance, but may not get chosen. I want you to know that God qualifies you and *he* is enough. He qualified you and chose you as soon as you made your first breath in this world. His qualification, endorsement, and recommendation trumps any resume, any cover letter, any job opportunity, any interview, any government assistance, any handout, any loan, and any*body* who you deem an opposer or even a hater. Your day is coming for you are qualified and chosen. A blessing too soon is indeed not a blessing at all. When God is ready, he'll open the door. If you're in a season of closed doors in terms of job opportunities, keep knocking because the father hears you and will open the doors (plural) in due season.

Questions:
1. Have you ever been qualified but not chosen for anything? How did it make you feel? How do you feel now?
2. What do you want God to do for you to qualify you for greater—not just on the job, but in life?
3. What can you do to qualify you for greater—not just on the job, but in life?

Prayer:
Father: I thank you now because I know greater is coming. I declare and decree that what qualifies me is enough for me to be chosen. I recognize that I was your first choice and because you qualified and chose me, I can walk with you into that interview, that new office, that new organization, that new opportunity and be chosen. I recognize that even if my resume does not qualify me, your relationship with me does. Thank you for the open door. In Jesus` name I pray. Amen.

THERE IS POWER IN A NAME

Hosea 1:4

Day 28

Hosea 1:4, *New Living Translation*

- *And the Lord said, name the child...*

Bill Clinton, the 42nd President of the United States, was a well-known Democrat. Many of his policies brought together both right-wing and left-wing politics, winning favor from both parties. Known as "The Big Dog", Clinton had an affair with White House Intern, Monica Lewinsky, leading to Clinton`s subsequent impeachment, forever tainting his name. Tiger Woods, ruler of the golf course, was known as one of the greatest golfers of all time. Referred to as Mr. T, he ruined his reputation and his name after he was caught cheating with New York City nightclub manager Rachel Uchitel. Bill Cosby, dubbed as "America's Dad" for his role in the Cosby Show where his charisma and character graced the screen and his life, suddenly became a disgrace after numerous women made sexual assault accusations against him by the mid 2010`s. This suit ruined the Cosby name and the network removed all reruns of the Cosby Show indefinitely. Will Smith, dubbed as the "Fresh Prince" and "Man in Black", allowed one bad decision of walking onto a worldwide stage and slapping Chris Rock to ultimately cause his demise, staining the greatest moment of his career and name. Once a beloved football player and actor, OJ`s legacy was forever changed after he was accused of murdering his ex-wife Nicole and her friend Ronald Goldman. The now infamous case, one of the biggest trials in the century, revealed OJ's history of domestic abuse. Though he was later proclaimed not guilty, he never returned to his former glory as advertisers and studios shied away from working with him again as they considered his name ruined. Each of these individuals may have committed acts that dropped their approval rating, their profound respect, their social status, or even their reputations. You see, in most cases it does not take but one act, one mishap, one hiccup, one strike, one mistake, one decision, one choice, or even one sin to ruin your name. There is power in a name.

The prophet Hosea lived in Israel about 200 years after Israel broke off from southern Judah as noted in 2nd Kings. In Hosea 1, God told Hosea to marry a prostitute named Gomer, using this scenario as a parallel to show how Israel acted like a prostitute in turning against the Lord, worshiping idols. They had three children. In biblical or even modern times, can you imagine the names the sons or daughters of a prostitute may be referred to by others? God instructed Hosea to name the eldest son Jezreel, symbolizing the punishment God would unleash on King Jezreel for the murders he committed at Jezreel. The eldest daughter was given the name Lo-ruhamah by God, meaning "not loved" for God will no longer show love to the people of Israel or forgive them. The youngest child's name would be La-ammi, meaning "not my people" as God declares Israel is not his people, and he is not their God. What name does God call you? Each of Hosea's children were given names symbolic of reality. What does your name say about you? I`m not referring to the name you were assigned at birth, but the names the Lord assigned to you. So often do characters on TV shows get named after their character: Superman, Maleficent, Grinch, Scrooge, Namor. Do you live up to the character God assigned you to be? If God named you right now based on your character, what might your name be now? Yesterday? Tomorrow?

There are several different names God assigns to us as being heirs to the lineage of his royalty: a new creation (2 Corinthians 5:17), a child of God (John 1:12), a friend of Jesus (John 15:15), justified and redeemed (Romans 3:24), a sanctified saint (1 Corinthians 1:2), a member of Christ's body (1 Corinthians 12:27), an ambassador for Christ (2 Corinthians 5:20), a temple of the Holy Spirit (1 Corinthians 6:19), chosen (Ephesians 1:4), redeemed and forgiven (Ephesians 1:7), made alive (Ephesians 2:4), saved (Ephesians 2:5), God's workmanship (Ephesians 2:10), a citizen of heaven (Philippians 3:20), and free (Galatians 5:1). How often do you represent the names God calls you?

In Shakespeare's play *Julius Caesar*, the people of Rome are trying to rid their King, Julius Caesar, as they feel he has grown too powerful and must be stopped. One of the characters named Cassius starts to realize that they should not be afraid of King Caesar as his name is no greater than anyone else`s. In layman's terms, he breathes the same air the townspeople breathe—making him no greater, no mightier, no better. Cassius says, "Brutus and Caesar...what's so special about the name Caesar? Why should that name be proclaimed more than yours? Write them together—yours is just as good a name. Pronounce them—it is just as nice to say. Weigh them—it's just as heavy. Cast spells with them and Brutus will call up a ghost as well as Caesar." We must realize that even when we do not live up to our names, Jesus lives up to his for he is Jehovah Jireh, Nissi, Shalom, and Rapha. He is the author and finisher of all things. He is the Son of the living God. He is the Wonderful Counselor, Mighty God, Everlasting Father, and Prince of Peace. He is the bright and Morning Star, Bridge over troubled water, and the Lily of the Valley. He is the Way, the Truth, and the Life. He is King of Kings and Lord of Lords. He is Alpha and Omega. He is a father to the fatherless and a mother to the motherless. He is our Rock, our Redeemer, our Savior, our keeper, and so much more. He lives up to his name every single day. How often do you live up to yours? There is power in a name. Live up to his name he assigned you for he lives up to his every day.

Questions:
1. If God named you right now based on your character (speech, thought, actions etc.), what might your name be now? Yesterday? Tomorrow?
2. Do you live up to the name God assigned you?
3. How can you live up to your name (given by God) daily?

Prayer:
Father: Help me to live up to my name you assigned me. You know the desires of my heart and the content of my character, but I ask that you lessen me and give me more of you. Help me to live up to my name as you have lived up to yours. And I know when I fall short, I can call on the name of Jesus to reset and restore our relationship to give me another chance to live up to what you call me. In Jesus` name I pray. Amen.

WHERE DO YOU CARRY YOUR BIBLE: IN HEART OR IN HAND?

Joel 2:13

Day 29

Joel 2:13, *New Living Translation*

- *Don't tear your clothing in your grief, but tear your hearts instead. Return to the Lord your God, for he is merciful and compassionate, slow to get angry and filled with unfailing love. He is eager to relent and not punish.*

In a song titled "Still in America" singer/songwriter Lecrae Devaughn Moore (known as Lecrae) writes of the issues plaguing 21st century America. He writes about the church, "Where church is a Broadway production for relevance" (Lecrae). The term "Broadway" originated in the late 1800`s, referring to theater productions, deemed the highest form of theatrical entertainment in the world coming in the forms of musicals, concerts, and lively events. More popularly, many know Broadway as a street located in New York, known as the heart of the American theatrical industry. These theaters seat a minimum of 500 people and so many people can see and be entertained by the show. What is interesting to note is that Broadway, today, has extended beyond the stage as it is beginning to take new life in television, film, music, and other forms of media, reaching not just the 500 people in attendance, but the entire world. If the 21st century church is indeed a "Broadway production for relevance", that would imply that the church of today finds purpose in presentation and not praise for God, it finds purpose in flamboyance and not the Father, it finds purpose in showiness and not in the Savior, it finds fame and influence in entertainment and not entering the kingdom. While this metaphor is one valid argument for the essence of the 21st century church, take a moment to identify your role in the production.

Joel, a prophet, is the author of this book of poetry, teaching and warning Israel that God's judgment is coming due to Israel's sin of disobedience and rebellion towards God. Early in the book, Joel places his focus on the day of the Lord, writing, "Let everyone tremble in fear because the day of the Lord is upon us. It is a day of darkness and gloom..." (Joel 2:1-2), referring to when the Lord will return and bring forth final judgment for the world. Because of this, Joel encourages the people to repent, saying, "Don't tear your clothing in your grief, but tear your hearts instead" (Joel 2:13, New Living Translation). It was custom in Jewish culture for people to tear their clothing in a time of mourning as an outward expression of hurt, pain, and grief. Joel knew that many would tear their clothing as an outward expression for all to see—putting on a Broadway production; yet, not tear their hearts by genuinely repenting inwardly—the tearing that truly matters. Charles Spurgeon once included a story in a sermon about a woman in sorrow who tore her clothes in repentance. Spurgeon read all ten commandments aloud to her so he could identify which ones she committed to cause her to act in such a manner. After reading all ten, the woman did not admit to breaking a single one, so Spurgeon assumed that the woman, confessing she committed no sin, tore her clothes as an outward act for the world to see. She tore her clothes outwardly, but did not tear her heart inwardly. Where do you carry your bible: in heart or in hand?

Are you a part of the show to entertain the audience or to serve and save yourself from the furnace of fire called hell? Are you a part of the show to boast and brag about your Sunday best attire for the audience to see or to boast and brag on the goodness of the Lord? Are you a part of the show to flip out, trip out, dance, or prance to mock the Holy Spirit for others to see or to simply be willing to let the Holy Spirit lead you as he pleases? Are you a part of the show to show the audience how much money you put in the church or to pay your tithes and offering as a duty to the kingdom? Lastly, are you a part of the show to throw your weight around because of your title or position in the ministry, or to live up to your title or position as a child of the Most-High king? I ask, where do you carry your bible: in heart or in hand? As humans we like to present a piece of ourselves for the world to see to *look* qualified and all-together, but just like God told Samuel, "The Lord does not look at the things people look at. People look at the outward appearance, but the Lord looks at the heart" (1 Samuel 16:7, New International Version). No need to flaunt your bible in your hand for people, but flaunt it in your heart for the Lord to see for it is he whose judgment matters, not the world.

Questions:
1. Where do you carry your bible: in heart or in hand?
2. What can you do daily to carry your bible more in your heart and less in your hand?

Prayer:
Father: Forgive me for all acts of outward appearance for the world to see. I realize that at times I carry my bible in my hand, but all you ask is that I carry it in my heart. Give me guidance, direction, and wisdom to show myself approved to you. In Jesus` name I pray. Amen.

LIONS AND TIGERS AND SNAKES, OH MY!

Amos 5:19

Day 30

Amos 5: 19, *New Living Translation*

- *In that day you will be like a man who runs from a lion— only to meet a bear. Escaping from the bear, he leans his hand against a wall in his house— and he's bitten by a snake.*

On August 25, 1939, the iconic and timeless movie *The Wizard of Oz* was released. Although many people today do not know the actors or actresses that played the various roles, people do know the major roles themselves, specifically: The Scarecrow, Tin Man, and the Cowardly Lion. After a brief deliberation about what they might see upon reaching Oz, Dorothy questions, "Do you suppose we'll meet any wild animals?" The Tin Man replies, "Uh, some but mostly lions and tigers and bears." In distress, Dorothy cries, "Oh! Lions and tigers and bears. Oh my!" as the trio skip away further on their journey, ironically running into the Cowardly Lion. To anyone displaced from home found in a strange land with unforeseen dangers on a journey never traveled before, the idea of seeing lions and tigers and bears may be a daunting one. Being three of the most ferocious animals on the planet, these carnivores would be of no match to our humanly tactics of survival or flight to escape their dangers. With no weapons or strategy to defend themselves, Dorothy and her three friends trek into the wilderness to Oz to find the Wizard, managing to avoid these dangers; but while *they* avoided such dangers, the day of the Lord is inevitable.

Amos was a biblical shepherd and fig tree farmer living in the land between northern Israel and Southern Judah during the reign of Jeroboam II—a king known for idol worship who also neglected the poor. God calls Amos to go to the city of Bethel to proclaim and announce God's word and the book is a compilation of his visions, sermons, and poems. Amos begins giving a voice to the poor, accusing the Israelites of ignoring the poor and having them in bondage. He continues, warning Israel of God's punishment due to their religious hypocrisy, idol worship, and sinful and unjust nature. Just like Joel, Amos informs the people of the day of the Lord, a period where God will return to exact justice and judgment on his people. Amos writes, "In that day you will be like a man who runs from a lion—only to meet a bear. Escaping from the bear, he leans his hand against a wall in his house—and he's bitten by a snake" (Amos, 5:19, New Living Translation). Other words Amos uses to describe the day of the Lord include "sorrowful, dark, and hopeless." In summary, Amos is stating that God sent you numerous prophets, but since you did not adhere to their warnings, the day of the Lord will inevitably prevail. Lions and tigers and snakes, oh my!

The day of the Lord is a day no man can escape. Even if we outrun the lion, escape the clutches of the bear, Amos tells us that even if we try to find refuge in our own homes—a place we deem as a safe-haven from the outside world—there too, will a snake find us and bite us. You can't run and you can`t hide. It does not matter if you`re black or white, rich or poor, educated or uneducated, a believer or an atheist, straight or bisexual, a president or a pastor, we all will have to answer to the Lord at his coming again. Because of this fact, we have to get on bended knees and pray for those who do not know Christ—that they establish a genuine relationship with him before it is too late. Jesus teaches his disciples, "So you, too, must keep watch! For you don`t know what day your Lord is coming" (Matthew 24:42, New Living Translation). "You also must be ready all the time, for the Son of Man will come when least expected" (Matthew 24: 44). If Jesus` disciples are not exempt from the day of the Lord, why do we think we will be? Lions and tigers and snakes are nothing compared to the fire and brimstone within the gates of hell. Repent (genuinely ask God for forgiveness) while the time is now!

Question:

1. How can you prepare yourself each day to be better prepared for the day of the Lord?

Prayer:

Father: Forgive me for all my sins. Help me to get my house in order for your coming. Lord, I realize you need no invitation for the day of your return is inevitable. I pray for those who do not yet have a relationship with you to establish one with you before it is too late. In Jesus` name I pray. Amen.

RETURN TO SENDER

Obadiah 1:20

Day 31

Obadiah 1:20, *New Living Translation*

- *The exiles of Israel will return to their land and occupy the Phoenician coast as far north as Zarephath. The captives from Jerusalem exiled in the north will return home and resettle the towns of the Negev.*

The phrase "return to sender" is used to describe mail that is processed, but later returned to the original sender for various reasons. Mail could be returned because the receiver refused to accept it, because the address was not found, or because it required signage and returned after multiple delivery attempts. Other reasons why mail may be labeled "return to sender" is due to an illegible address, insufficient postage, or a mistake caused by the carrier in the delivery process. Putting this in a more realistic context, Elvis Presley wrote a song called "Return to Sender" which tells of a man who sent a letter to his lover, but it later returned to him with her writing on it stating, "Return to sender / Address unknown / No such number / No such zone." Presley writes that they did have a quarrel, but he wrote on the letter "I`m sorry, but my letter keeps coming back", assigning responsibility on the letter and not the woman. He then decides to place it in the mailbox, sending it "special delivery", yet the letter returns with the same hand-written message. Finally, the man decides to hand-deliver the letter to her stating, "If it comes back the next day / Then I'll understand." The song ends: (The writing on it) / Return to sender/ Return to Sender." How often do you think the Devil sends attacks to us with the intention to steal, kill, and destroy and God hits "return to sender?"

Obadiah is the shortest book of the Old Testament and is a series of judgment poems against a place called Edom, a neighboring city to Israel. Edom and Israel shared an ancestry, but when the Babylonians conquered Israel, the Edomites did not assist Israel, but rather helped the Babylonians capture and kill Israelite refugees due to the longstanding feud amongst Israel and Edom. Essentially, the Edomites kicked the Israelites while they were down. Obadiah, a prophet, seeks to hold Edom accountable due to the pride they possessed in the destruction of their own people. Just like Amos, Obadiah also mentions the day of the Lord, but offers a greater sense of hope near the end of the book. He writes, "But Jerusalem...will be a holy place. And the people of Israel will come back to reclaim their inheritance" (Obadiah 1: 17, New Living Translation). Obadiah is prophesying a restored kingdom of God built on faithfulness, which will later expand to nations around "New Israel". Not only will the Isrealites come back, but "the exiles of Israel will return to their land" and the "captives from Jerusalem exiled in the north will return home" (Obadiah 1: 20, New Living Translation).

The word "return" strikes me with a sense of power and authority in Scripture. The "return" key on a computer typically has the same function as "enter." It allows you to create a new line when typing, however the word "return" in Scripture has a dual-function not offered on computers. Not only did God hit "return" by sending the Devil's attack back to him by allowing the Israelites to return to the land that was once theirs, but God grants them a fresh start, a new opportunity, a new "line". What the Devil meant for evil, God turned it around for their good. If God did it for them, he can surely do it for you. The Israelites lost everything, but God turned their exile or exit into an entrance back into what once belonged to them. When devilish attacks arise in your life, return it to the sender in the pits of hell using the authority Jesus already gave: "I have given you authority over all the power of the enemy, and you can walk among snakes and scorpions and crush them. Nothing will injure you" (Luke 10:19, New Living Translation). Return the attack to the sender and wait for God to deliver his gift—the one that keeps on giving.

Questions:
1. What attacks have recently arrived at your "doorstep?"
2. How can you use your power and authority given by God to return "packages" to Satan, the sender?
3. What can you do in the future to prepare for packages Satan plans to send?

Prayer:
Father: I declare and decree that any attack the Devil is waiting to dispatch over my life, that it be canceled, uprooted, destroyed and returned back to the sender in the name of Jesus! Help me to walk in the power and authority you have granted me. I speak a return on everything the Devil stole from me—not just a return on what he took, but an abundance and an overflow in addition to it. In Jesus` name I pray. Amen.

MEET "MR.NICE GUY"

Jonah 4:2

Day 32

Jonah 4: 2, *New Living Translation*

- *So he complained to the Lord about it: "Didn't I say before I left home that you would do this, Lord? That is why I ran away to Tarshish! I knew that you are a merciful and compassionate God, slow to get angry and filled with unfailing love. You are eager to turn back from destroying people.*

The book of Jonah is filled with several stereotypical characters—characters who fit predictable, ironic, or clichéd molds. Jonah features a rebellious prophet (Jonah), soft-hearted sailors, and a humble king of a powerful empire. These three characters are the most prevalent stereotypes within the book, but there is another: a "Mr. Nice Guy." While the origins of the phrase "no more Mr. Nice Guy" is questionable, it refers to a person who may be deemed a pushover, passive, weak, too nice, or even too forgiving. It could mean someone who offers too many chances or absorbs hurt from others or ill-treatment from others but forgives them each time. Likewise, the phrase "no more Mr. Nice Guy" marks the end of one`s passive or pushover nature. It's when enough is enough, as this person puts an end to being taken advantage of. As an educator, I know I`m a "Mr. Nice Guy". I give too many warnings, too many chances, too many opportunities of redemption that students sometimes fail to take me seriously. I exhibit a very "short-term memory" when it comes to ill-behaved students and I am extremely forgiving. Although no student has directly told me this, I know they would classify me as a "Mr. Nice Guy." But, this stereotypical title does not qualify me as a pushover, passive, weak, too nice, or even too forgiving; however, it does qualify me as being Godly.

Jonah is a renowned biblical character. God told Jonah, a prophet, to go to Nineveh to preach against their evil and injustices. Jonah decides to run away, landing himself on a ship. Believing Jonah has caused them misfortune in running into a storm, the sailors ask Jonah how he wants to leave: willingly or forcefully. Jonah is thrown overboard; God sends a whale, which swallows him up. But it is in the whale, where Jonah prays to God, telling him he`ll obey God forever and go to Nineveh as he was previously instructed. Jonah complies by telling the people the message from God. The Ninevites fast, pray, and turn from all violence. The bible writes, "When God saw what they had done and how they had put a stop to their evil ways, he changed his mind and did not carry out the destruction he had threatened" (Jonah 3:1, New Living Translation). This act angered Jonah, revealing his true intentions for fleeing from the assignment God gave him. In summary, Jonah says he fled because he knew God is "merciful, compassionate, slow to anger and filled with unfailing love" (Jonah 4:2). He knew God would forgive him. It's almost like sinning because you know God will forgive you (if you are contrite). Jonah took advantage of God's mercy—a common act imposed on "Mr. Nice Guys." God responds, asking Jonah the same question repeatedly: Is it right for you to be angry because of *my* mercy?" In layman's terms, God is stating that his mercy exists to save and offer multiple chances to those living in spiritual darkness; so how can *you*, Jonah, be angry about a positive quality of *me*, God? It's almost like getting angry with a soda machine when you pay for one and two comes out. Jonah`s displaced and misplaced anger is not sensical and God wants him to realize it.

The bible declares us "uniquely and wonderfully made." For some, it may be easy to rule with an iron fist, with sternness and assertiveness. For others, God wired us with grace, mercy, and "Mr. Nice Guy-ness." For every person out there reading this, never, ever, *ever* feel guilty or "less than" because of your "Mr. Nice Guy-ness" for I, too, am a victim. That's what the enemy wants you to believe. Having this trait of "Mr. Nice Guy-ness" *makes* you Godly. God is not a God of a second chance, but another chance. Jonah, the Israelites, Moses, David, Peter, humanity—all receive or received not a second chance, but another chance and another and another. God in his infinite power has the ability to discipline us as he pleases after the first mishap or mistake, but he chooses grace and mercy. Today, choose grace. Choose mercy. If we expect God to establish a "Mr. Nice Guy-ness" with us, we need to establish a "Mr. Nice Guy-ness" first with ourselves, then with others. (70*7: IYKYK).

Questions:

1. Is it right for you to be unforgiving and merciless when you serve a merciful God who is slow to anger and quick to forgive?
2. Do you classify yourself as being representative of "Mr. Nice-Guy-ness?"
3. How can you be more merciful in your daily lives? Why is it important to extend mercy?

Prayer:

Father: thank you for being a God not of a second chance, but another chance. I thank you for your grace, your mercy, your compassion, but most importantly your unfailing love. Help me to extend mercy to those who need it, just as you have showered me with mercy every day, for every day your mercies are new. In Jesus` name I pray. Amen.

PAY UP!

Micah 3:11

Day 33

Micah 3:11, *New Living Translation*

- *You rulers make decisions based on bribes; you priests teach God's laws only for a price; you prophets won't prophesy unless you are paid.*

Money: brings us together, tears us apart. The bible writes, "For the love of money is the root of all evil" (1st Timothy 6:10, King James Version). The idea of the destructive forces of money appear frequently in society: in TV, movies, social media, literature, and even within the transactions and necessities of life. The typical human being usually does not gripe about the money we earn on our paychecks from our careers or the money we earn on other forms of income we've worked for, but the second we loan our money to someone in need or have to pay for something (whether it is a bill or service), troubles often arise. This is commonplace and understandable for it is money and the economy that affects not only us, but conversely for the ones in which we love and provide. Money is so dominant and controlling as so many things we hold near and dear to us within our lives often relate or stem from our finances: health (mental and physical) and wellness, family and friends, education, time, love (or versions of it), purpose and passion, memories, and even simply existing (bills, services, taxes). Regardless of the nature and interest of money, in order to live we have to "pay up." My question is, to whom do you pay and why?

Micah warned the Israelites of the impending destruction of Assyria and Babylon. What is unique about this book is that Micah places the emphasis of God`s contempt on the Israelite leaders. Micah chapter 2 focuses on these accusations, calling the Israelite leaders evil, thieves, fraudulent and violent, cheaters, replying that "I [God] will reward your evil with evil" (Micah 2:3, New Living Translation). The word 'reward' is a unique one as one may think that evil can`t be rewarded because it's evil; however, the Israelite leaders deemed their evil ways as rewarding as they profited from the poor to become wealthy. America is a repeat of biblical times in this regard as the wealthy feed off the poor: the poor get poorer and the rich get richer. In chapter 3, Micah continues his accusations writing, "Listen, you leaders of Israel! You are supposed to know right from wrong..." (Micah 3:1, New Living Translation). Leaders are deemed the reflection of the business, establishment, organization, district, state, providence, or even country. People typically flock to or leave jobs because of the leadership represented and the skills and qualities they exemplify or lack. Micah continues, "You rulers make decisions based on bribes; you priests teach God's law only for a price; you prophets won`t prophesy unless you are paid" (Micah 3:11, New Living Translation). In other words, Micah is asking "who do you really work for, money or for the Lord?" These leaders were taking advantage of the people, using their gifts only at the expense of receiving payment.

The term "pay up" is just as important to the giver as it is the receiver. The phrase is defined as giving money to someone that you owe. My question again is, givers, to whom do you pay and why? Do you pay outwardly to man or upwardly to God? Do you pay out to be accepted or pay up for the kingdom and kingdom building? Do you pay God what is right or what is left? The bible writes in Malachi, "Bring the full amount of your tithes to the Temple. Put me to the test and you will see that I will open the windows (plural) of heaven and pour out on you in abundance all kinds of good things" (Malachi 3:10, Good News Translation). If you give God his 10% first, he`ll stretch the other 90% in your favor. "You must give willingly and not reluctantly, for God loves a cheerful giver" (2 Corinthians 9:7). Your payment does not always have to be in terms of money. It can be in time, talent, or even service. Now, for receivers: my question is, from whom do you take and why? Do you take for the uplifting of your status and the depressing of others? Do you take for your fulfillment or to help fill God's kingdom? Do you take as a means to remain tightfisted or do you take to give to those in need? Society is filled with givers and takers, but make sure that your giving and taking is to pay up for the kingdom of God, to pay up to salvation, to pay up on your down payment on your mansion in heaven, and to pay up for his glory. God is well-deserving of your payment. Pay up!

Questions:
1. Would you deem yourself more of a giver or a taker?
2. Do you tithe properly? If not, how can you begin to tithe (giving 10% of income) appropriately?
3. Do you give and take for the edification of yourself, others, or God?

Prayer:
Father: Help me to give and receive with a heart for you. Incline my heart to pay up for you and not pay up for myself or others. Help me not to exhibit the behavior of the Israelite leaders but allow me to do *everything* for the uplifting of you and the representation of your kingdom. In Jesus` name I pray. Amen.

CAUTION: BEWARE CLAPPING

Nahum 3:19

Day 34

Nahum 3:19, *New International Version*

- *Nothing can heal you; your wound is fatal. All who hear the news about you clap their hands at your fall, for who has not felt your endless cruelty?*

The practice of clapping dates back at least to the ancient Greeks as audiences applauded at performances they conducted as a form of entertainment. Clapping acts as a visual and an auditory signal that occurs involuntarily (i.e. when someone is surprised) or voluntarily. Psychology argues that there are six major reasons why people applaud, or clap and the first is an applause of astonishment. It is this kind of clap people do when they are startled or surprised. The second type is a playful clap when we are listening or clapping along to the rhythm of music or singing. The third type of clap is one of motivation. Seeing that someone is nervous or afraid to speak or act in public, tugs at our heart`s emotional strings leading us to clap to encourage that person's effort. The fourth is a recognitional applause, which typically occurs at the end of a performance, as a team enters or departs from their field, court, or arena. It is the clap that says "we support you" at the beginning, throughout, and even at the end of the game. The fifth type is a protocol applause—the kind of clap that occurs after someone gives a speech, conducts a performance, or receives an award. The last kind of clap is an ironic clap that expresses sarcasm, displeasure after a poor performance, usually consisting of a slow, less rhythmic tempo. What I find interesting is that you never truly know the nature or intention behind someone's clap. Visually speaking, *all* claps seem supportive, emerging from a place of good intention, but that is not always the case. Caution: Beware clapping.

The book of Nahum features one of these clapping methods. The book is a collection of poems that reveal the downfall of Assyria (capital: Nineveh—where God sent Jonah). Assyria had grown destructive and violent and were deemed reckless and out-of-proportion. The book is written in a gloomy tone as Nahum recounts a history of violence and war and oppression and its effect on the innocent. Similarly, in Marvel Studio`s *Avengers: Civil War,* the "government" placed checks and balances on the Avengers (a group of heroes) recognizing their heroic efforts in saving countless individuals, but bringing attention to the innocent individuals lost as collateral damage in the crossfire. Nahum`s purpose is to show that God cares about the innocent and grieves for them as he will orchestrate the downfall of the violent and destructive nations. Nahum 2 details the fall of Assyria as Nahum 3 shows the results. The book ends with the death of the king of Assyria—not a member of the "innocent." In summary, Nahum writes to the dying king, "Your shepherds are asleep, your princes lie dead in the dust, your people are scattered" (Nahum 3:18, New Living Translation). He continues, "Nothing can heal you; your wound is fatal. All who hear the news about you clap their hands at your fall" (Nahum 3:19, New International Version). This clap was not one of astonishment, not one of playfulness, not one of motivation, not one of recognition, not one of protocol, nor one of ironic intent, it was one of praise and celebration at the expense of one's downfall. While the people may or may not have been wrong in their desire to clap, why are people clapping for you? Caution: Beware clapping.

Everyone that claps for or at you, smiles at you, praises you, hugs you, offers you a handshake, or even acknowledges you is not *for* you. Visually speaking it may look like the entire world is your oyster, and that everyone is in your corner or in your pocket, but in reality only a heart of discernment and wisdom can detect the true supporters from the true haters. We have to be so careful who we share our life with, our milestones, our experiences, our moments of greatness, our favor. We have to be so cautious in our talking because just because someone is willing to listen, does not mean they *care* to listen. They may listen in your face, clap at your performance, and rate you poorly behind closed doors. Just because someone is available, does not mean they *care* to avail themself to you. They may watch your act, applaud at your performance, then gossip and criticize you behind closed doors. Every friend on Facebook is not your fan. Every trip is not for Twitter. Every instance is not for Instagram. Every shoutout is not for Snapchat. The more people know about you—whether good or bad—the more ammunition they have to pray and prey your downfall—for every applause is not grounded in good intention. If you want to applaud, applaud for God first, then for yourself. You both deserve it. Caution: Beware clapping!

Questions:

1. When do you clap?
2. For whom do you clap?
3. Why do you clap?

Prayer:

Father: Thank you for your insight. I pray that you give me eyes and ears of discernment to show me the true nature and intention of those who clap for me. Help me to not seek approval from them. The only approval that matters, is approval from you Lord. Thank you for giving me your stamp of approval. In Jesus` name I pray. Amen.

POSITION, PATIENCE, AND PERSPECTIVE
Habakkuk 2:1

Day 35

Habakkuk 2:1, *International Standard Version*

- *I will stand at my guard post and station myself on a tower. I will wait and see what the Lord will say about me and what I will answer when he reprimands me.*

2nd Timothy 2:5 writes, "And athletes cannot win the prize unless they follow the rules" (New Living Translation). No matter the sport whether it be the more popular ones like football, basketball, or baseball, individual ones like swimming, boxing, or golfing, or other less popular sports such as track and field, hockey, soccer, or tennis; each of these sports have their own unique set of written rules to play the game. Written rules include the amount of people that should be in the game at any given time, the time each quarter lasts, or even scoring protocol. Within every sport, there are also several unwritten rules. Examples of these include not scoring in your own goal, not showing up other players in an overly-arrogant manner, or showboating or scoring within the last seconds of a basketball game when everyone is leisurely waiting for the game to conclude. While these unwritten rules are more common, there are three others that are even more unwritten: position, patience, and perspective. Approaching *any* sport with being in the proper position, having adequate patience, and possessing the proper perspective or mindset will—in most cases—yield a win for you or your team. This same unwritten rule of proper position, patience, and perspective can be applied spiritually to yield results from our Father, which art in heaven.

Habakkuk, another minor prophet, lived in the final decade of Israel's southern kingdom. What is interesting to note about his words, is that none of them are addressed to Israel, but *only* to God. He struggles with how a good God can allow so much evil to exist in their world, referencing the evil, violent, and destructive nature of Babylon and Assyria. The book consists of poems of lament as Habakkuk complains to God about the evil he has witnessed. His first complaint is against the Israelite leaders as Habakkuk questions God, asking why he isn't doing anything with the evil-doing leaders of Israel. God informs Habakkuk that he is aware of their actions and tells him the armies of Babylon are his instrument to punish the Israelites. Stemming from this argument, Habakkuk's second complaint is centered around the fact that Babylon`s evil is worse than that of the Israelites as Habakkuk questions how can a holy God use such a corrupt nation to execute justice. As Habakkuk awaits God's response, the bible writes that Habakkuk did three things: stood at his post on the tower, waited on God`s response, and listened for correction. Habakkuk practiced the unwritten rule of prayer: position, patience, perspective. Habakkuk stood at the top of his tower. As you know, the higher you are, the more ground you can visually see—the more area you can assess. Habakkuk stood in a position high enough to see God coming. Secondly, he waited. Oftentimes we pray to God and move on without giving God the necessary time (not our time, but his) to respond. Habakkuk waited patiently. Thirdly, Habakkuk approached God with proper perspective, expecting God to correct or reprimand him. When we pray we often come to God in a state of guiltlessness as if we don't have anything we need to be forgiven of *or* as if we have all the answers when we barely ask God the right questions.

When we approach the throne of grace, we must approach it rightly. We have to come to our father on bended knees with our hands interlocked. We have to be patient and wait for his response. So many of us (even I do at times) make the mistake of saying "Amen" and going on about our day, not giving God the wait time necessary to see if he has anything to tell us. Because we live in a "microwave" age, we like to take things in our own hands instead of waiting on God to preheat, bake, and take our blessing out the oven putting it on our tables. Thirdly, we have to approach God with proper perspective. We have to humble ourselves before the king, acting as if we have things in our lives that need reprimanding or correcting. The bible tells us that "all have sinned and fall short of the glory of God" (Romans 3:23, New International Version). Come to God correctly. Assume the position, wait patiently, approach with proper perspective, and your prayer life will improve so that you can win "the game." (Be sure to tell God thank you).

Questions:

1. In your prayer life, do you approach God with proper position, patience, and perspective?
2. What "P" do you need to improve? How can you improve it effectively?

Prayer:

Father: Forgive me for not always approaching you properly. Help me to position myself for optimal results. Grant me the ability to wait on you and listen for your still, small voice. Incline my heart to approach you with a humble and contrite heart, for that is the approach that yields favor. In Jesus` name I pray.

COOKED TO PERFECTION

Zephaniah 3:8-9

Day 36

Zephaniah 3: 8-9, *English Standard Version*

- *Therefore, be patient," says the Lord. "Soon I will stand and accuse these evil nations. For I have decided to gather the kingdoms of the earth and pour out my fiercest anger and fury on them. All the earth will be devoured by the fire of my jealousy. "Then I will purify the speech of all people, so that everyone can worship the Lord together.*

One of the most popular grilling techniques is that of charring, meaning burning something slightly or partly. One misconception is that charring can only occur on the grill, but it can be accomplished on the stovetop or by broiling it in the oven. Charring imparts a smoky flavor on foods giving it a heightened taste of pleasant bitterness. Foods that are typically charred are usually meats such as ribs, chicken, smoked sausages, or burger patties; or vegetables such as corn, carrots, or bell peppers. Not only do these foods taste a little better when charred, they add a more appealing look physically, especially when cooked outdoors on a grill. On the contrary, we all have that uncle that takes grilling beyond charring. The uncle that mans the grill at *every* cookout that may get sidetracked, grilling the food a bit too long, surpassing charred and becoming burned. While burned foods are considered cooked past the point of being edible, charred foods offer culinary value in their methodical approach. Further, burning usually occurs accidentally, while charring occurs intentionally. How would you like your meat cooked?

Zephaniah, the prophet, lived in the final decade of southern Judah and this book is a collection of his poetry. Early in the book, Zepheniah paints an apocalyptic picture of the Lord's coming again, describing how the world will end. Interestingly, Zephaniah does not mention whose army will bring forth God's justice as that is not his focus; he intends to highlight God`s role in orchestrating the rise and fall of locations contingent to their actions toward him. In the second chapter, Zephaniah turns his attention to the judgment of nations and Jerusalem to show the widespread nature of corruption and arrogance in the land. However, just like the other prophets, Zephaniah closes the book with a semblance of hope in an atypical way. He writes the Lord will "gather the kingdoms of the earth and pour out [his] fiercest anger and fury on them. All the earth will be devoured by the fire of [his] jealousy" (Zephaniah 3:8, English Standard Version). If one stopped reading here, "fire" is connoted as a burning leading to destruction and death. Zephaniah continues, "Then I will purify the speech of all people, so that everyone can worship the Lord together" (Zephaniah 3:9, English Standard Version), connoting that the kind of fire the Lord will send is a fire of purification, not destruction. It is a fire of refinement, not deterioration. It is a fire intended for growth, not death. It is a fire of building up, not tearing down. How would you like your meat cooked?

When we experience the "fiery trials" of life we sometimes view them as God's way of punishing us for sin. Have you ever considered that those trials might simply be crash tests of our life to test our strength and improve our character in Jesus? Before cars are released they are first tested with a variety of tests, completely dismantling and demolishing their structure just to test the strength and durability of the final project. These tests are conducted so designers and engineers can tweak aspects of the vehicle to improve its overall quality. Have you considered that God is just conducting a quality control test on your life as you go through your "fiery trials?" The fire that God sends is not intended to hurt, harm, endanger, or discourage you, but rather to strengthen, uplift, encourage, and better you for a more faithful walk with him. Don`t think that God is trying to burn you as punishment, he is burning off any and every part of you that is not like him. Greed: burn it off, God. Envy: burn it off, God. Lust: burn it off, God. Pride: burn it off, God. Anger: burn it off, God. Anything that is not like you, burn it off, God. Make me new; make me over. Cook me to perfection. I realize now that when you turn the temperature up in my life, it is for the making and not the breaking. How would you like your meat cooked? Not rare, not medium rare, not medium, not medium well, not burned, but charred and well done, "my good and faithful servant" (Matthew 25:21, New Living Translation).

Questions:

1. What are some instances when God turned the heat up in your life?
2. Looking back, what did you learn or how did you grow from this temperature change?
3. From what do you need to be purified or refined?
4. How would you like your meat cooked?

Prayer:

Father: Cook me to perfection in your eyes. Do whatever it takes to make me more like you. Help me to adjust to the fiery trials in my life and never, ever allow me to deem them as a means of punishment, but a means of purification. In Jesus` name I pray. Amen.

THE FUTURE IS IN YOUR HANDS

Haggai 2:13

Day 37

Haggai 2:13, *New Living Translation*

- *Then Haggai asked, "If someone becomes ceremonially unclean by touching a dead person and then touches any of these foods, will the food be defiled?" And the priests answered, "Yes."*

"What do you want to be when you grow up?" An elementary school student may respond a firefighter, a pro athlete, a scientist, or an astronaut. When approaching a middle school student, it is commonplace to ask, "Are you ready for high school?" Most of them say "no" only because they are already turned off by school, but sometimes you do get an emphatic "yes", as they are intrigued by the sense of newness: new friends, new classes, a new environment, and even themselves transforming into a new being. When approaching a high schooler we ask, "What are your plans after graduation?" Students typically respond one of four ways: military, college, workforce, or "I don`t know." It is those "I don`t know" responses that worry not only the person asking the question, but also to the student responding. We often assume that at this day and stage in life, especially as a high school senior, that students have their post-secondary options identified and have a plan in place for getting there. It is those "I don't knows" that escalate the interrogation process: "What do you like to do?" What have you considered?" and even "Where do you see yourself in five years?" No matter the responses students give regardless of their educational level and status (elementary, middle, high, college, postgraduate), the one piece of advice that may offer semblance is: the future is in your hands.

Haggai is a prophet who exists 70 years after the exile following the fall of Babylon. Persia had become the new world leader and any exiled Jews were allowed to return under the leadership of Joshua (high priest) and Zerubbabel (heir of David). Early in the book, Haggai writes of accusations against the Israelites as they returned home building their own luxurious homes while the temple of the Lord was yet to be rebuilt. Surprisingly, the Israelites listened due to the fear of God and they began work in rebuilding the temple. Haggai chapter 2 resumes one month later as the Israelites rebuilt the temple, although they built it merely for the sake of building it. They built it haphazardly and in a desultory (lacking a plan or enthusiasm) manner, nothing like the former, immaculate temple of Solomon. Later in the chapter, Haggai reflects and teaches a lesson on this lack of effort, writing, "If someone becomes ceremonially unclean by touching a dead person and then touches any of these foods, will the food be defiled?" And the priests answered, "Yes" (Haggai 2:13, New Living Translation). Haggai is trying to illustrate that our touch can lead to our demise, much like sin. What have you touched lately? Haggai then reminds the people of the shortcomings they experienced while effortlessly building the temple, showing why all their work had gone in vain ("they refused to return to the Lord") for their heart and priorities were in the wrong places. But, Haggai offers hope in redirecting the people's priorities stating, "from this day onward I will bless you" (Haggai 2:19, New Living Translation). Why? Because the Lord has shown them through Haggai that their priorities were not in order, but once they build with the intent of giving God their best, God will see their hearts and bless them. In other words, their future is in their hands, literally. The better they build the Temple under good intentions, the better and greater blessings the Lord will bestow upon them.

What does the touch of your hands say about your future? This touch does not have to be your work, but it can be people, places, or even sin itself. Is your future bright or bleak? The future is in your hands. Haggai is teaching that we cannot do any work for God unless our heart is in the right place. We can't treat God like a toolbox, only pulling it out when things need fixing in our lives, but we need to make him the priority tool that we use to fix our lives every day: a tool that can fix any leak, tighten any loose bolt, drive nails we need strengthening, cover open holes or unresolved trauma, cut away things that are not like him, sand away our sin, or even haul us away from the attacks of hell. The bible says, "So whether you eat or drink or whatever you do, do it *all* for the glory of God" (1 Corinthians 10:31, New Living Translation)—not the glory of men, the glory of the world, nor the glory of you. The bible doesn't say "some" or a certain day or days of the week; we must put God first and foremost all the time for it is our touch with him that will brighten our future. Sometimes all it takes is a little adjusting and tweaking to get our priorities in order and it is a pursuit we must pursue daily with intention and purpose. The choice is yours for the future is in your hands. Wash your "hands" because the future depends on it.

Questions:

1. What do your hands say about you?
2. What have you touched that could make your hands "dirty?" What have you touched that could make your hands "clean?"
3. Where does God and your spirituality lie on your priority list? How can you keep God as your number one every day?

Prayer:

Father: My life is in your hands. All I need is a touch from you. Touch my responsibilities and allow me to always make you my number one priority. Help me to refrain from touching anything that is not like you for the future is in my hands. Just like you promised the Israelites a "New Jerusalem", grant me a new me. I thank you for my future of new. Father, let me never lose touch with you. In Jesus` name I pray. Amen.

MAXIMUM OCCUPANCY

Zechariah 2:4

Day 38

Zechariah 2:4, *New Living Translation*

- *The other angel said, "Hurry, and say to that young man, 'Jerusalem will someday be so full of people and livestock that there won't be room enough for everyone! Many will live outside the city walls.*

The term *maximum occupancy* refers to the maximum number of people permitted within a building, structure, or vehicle at any given moment. Maximum occupancy exists for the safety and security of all members present within a space in case of emergency to provide a smoother, more efficient means of comfort, space, and escape for all members involved. Signs that display this number must be present, maintained, legible, and placed in a suitable location. Maximum occupancy is calculated by dividing the area of a room by its prescribed amount of space per individual. Dormitories tend to require 50 square feet of floor area per occupant, elevators require about two square feet per occupant—about six square feet per occupant for a stadium, about six square feet for a passenger on a plane, and about four square feet for riders of a school bus. Studies show that individuals need between 200-400 square feet of space to live comfortably in any given space. Even in the housing market, there are zoning laws and regulations that place quotas on distances between homes, buildings, and other structures for the optimal comfortability of all members involved. Despite these facts, God was the only approval Jerusalem needed to exist with over maximum occupancy.

In the book of Zechariah, we see the continued effort of the Israelites to rebuild God's temple after the return of the exiles from Babylon to Jerusalem. Along with Haggai, Zechariah motivated the people to set their priorities in order, putting their hearts and effort into the rebuilding. The book is filled with several visions of Zechariah regarding the actions, attitudes, and arrival of God's New Jerusalem, where God would pour out his spirit on them all, bringing healing, restoration, and renewal to the land. In Zechairah`s third vision, a man has a measuring stick in his hand as he is preparing to measure Jerusalem for the coming of God's people and the fulfillment of God's kingdom. An angel appeared and told the man, "Hurry, Jerusalem will someday be so full of people and livestock that there won't be room enough for everyone!" (Zechariah 2:4, New Living Translation) to the point that many will have to live outside the city walls. God is illustrating that his spirit will be poured out amongst so many people that they all will not be contained in this New Jerusalem. They may not be comfortable. But, how many of you know that you sometimes have to be uncomfortable before you can be comfortable. That mattress, that car seat, that new position, that recliner, that new home, that new partner, that new shoe, or even that new "(hair)do" may feel uncomfortable at first, but the more you acclimate yourself to it, the more comfortable it becomes.

I find revelation in this Scripture for just like the coming of the New Jerusalem, we all desire new: new friends, new relationships, new encounters. We desire new promotions, new opportunities, new positions. We desire to embark on new adventures, see new places, and try new foods. We desire new favor, new blessings, and new levels of spirituality. We desire new cars, new clothes, new devices. Reading Haggai`s devotional we learn how to prioritize our priorities, but Zechariah teaches us the fruitfulness of getting our priorities in order and it can be summed up in one word: maximum. Max: the highest setting on an amplifier. Max: the highest pressure of heating or air flow. Max: the highest altitude of an aircraft. Max: the highest grade on an assignment. Max: the highest credit score possible. Max: the most money you can withdraw. We serve a God that "does the most" and by no means do I mean that negatively. God is preparing to do such a new thing that you`ll think you can't contain it. Your maximum is not God`s maximum for he has no limit, no quota, no restriction, no ceiling, nor no bounds. The man who measured Jeruslaem did it in vain. We become so focused in trying to measure our lives and our blessings, while God is trying to teach us to throw the tape measure away for no tape measure or ruler can match his might. He can do "exceedingly, abundantly, above all we can ask or think" (Ephesians 3:20, New King James Version). God is going to give you such great vision that people will laugh at its magnitude. But if God can deliver the most sinful, the most rebellious, the most faithless, and the most stubborn individuals called the Israelites, why think he has exempted you for giving you not just the maximum in your eyes, but the maximum in his. Believe it. Receive it. Make room.

Questions:
1. What are you measuring in your life right now?
2. What are you making room to receive from God?

Prayer:
Father: I thank you for expectation. I ask that you loose the restrictions I place on my vision, loose the restrictions I place on my purpose, loose the restrictions I place on my ability, loose the restrictions I place on my gifts, loose the restrictions I place on my grace, loose the restrictions I place on you. I ask that you release not my version of maximum, but your version in due time. In Jesus` name I pray. Amen.

A CURSED BLESSING

Malachi 2:2

Day 39

Malachi 2:2, *New Living Translation*

- *Listen to me and make up your minds to honor my name," says the Lord of Heaven's Armies, "or I will bring a terrible curse against you. I will curse even the blessings you receive. Indeed, I have already cursed them, because you have not taken my warning to heart.*

A family tree goes beyond names and lineage. On paper the names are merely that: names. But what does your family tree say about you? I`m not referring to the obvious such as "You look just like your mom" or "you have hair just like your father." Look beyond the heredity and look for the spiritual. What commonalities can be traced throughout your family tree? Do you find traces of blessings such as generational wealth, property, or businesses or do you find traces of curses such as poverty, drug abuse, or adultery? God knows not just you, but he knows where you came from: God and Abraham and Isaac and Jacob down to your parents of "great", your parents, all the way down to you, your children, and their continual lineage. The 28th chapter of Deuteronomy features not only blessings, but many generational curses. Most common curses include those aforementioned, in addition to sexual abuse, violence, alcoholism, depression, mental illness, suicide, destructive attitudes, godlessness and many others. Each of these can be the result of a generational curse. When we think of "curses" we typically think of those infamous swear words or things cast by wizards and witches, failing to realize just as God blesses, the Devil curses.

Malachi, the last of the Minor Prophets, lived about 100 years after the Israelites returned from the Babylonian exile. Malachi's message was centered on the people who remained in Jerusalem despite the exile and return by many. After God advised the Israelites to put their priorities in order, the Israelites rebuilt the temple, yet things still were not going well. It becomes evident that the Israelites who repopulated were just as unfaithful as their ancestors, causing their family tree to remain spiritually stagnant. The Israelites dispute different matters with God such as asking God questions concerning God's love for them, God's justice and judgment on them, God`s alleged neglect, God`s alleged betrayal, and God`s superfluous nature as the Israelites believe God has done nothing for them. Early in the book, God addresses the priests—the leaders—for their inability to lead by example. God says, "Listen to me and make up your minds to honor my name," says the LORD of Heaven's Armies, "or I will bring a terrible curse against you. I will curse even the blessings you receive. Indeed, I have already cursed them, because you have not taken my warning to heart" (Malachi 2:2, New Living Translation). When you think about a priest, many consider them to be people with *all* the answers and with *zero* issues; but they are humans, just like the common man. We are all one-in-the-same within the body of Christ. God is reprimanding the priests for their unrighteous deeds, writing that even their blessings will be curses. On the surface, this may sound perplexing and contradictory, such as saying a number can be both positive and negative for these are antonyms just like blessings and curses. Perhaps God is referring to perspective. Things in our lives we deem as blessings, end up truly being curses. For example, having a child (blessing), who grows up battling suicide (curse) or getting a promotion (blessing) that causes us to push God further down on our priority list (curse) due to working longer hours. But, there is hope for curses are made to be broken.

Just as curses come through the bloodline it can be canceled by blood: the blood of Jesus. Because Jesus is our sacrifice of atonement, curses are paid by his blood. Deuteronomy 30:15-19 writes, "Now listen! Today I am giving you a choice between life and death, between prosperity and disaster. For I command you this day to love the Lord your God and to keep his commands, decrees, and regulations by walking in his ways. If you do this, you will live and multiply, and the Lord your God will bless you and the land you are about to enter and occupy. But if your heart turns away and you refuse to listen, and if you are drawn away to serve and worship other gods, then I warn you now that you will certainly be destroyed. You will not live a long, good life in the land you are crossing the Jordan to occupy. Today I have given you the choice between life and death, between blessings and curses. Now I call on heaven and earth to witness the choice you make. Oh, that you would choose life, so that you and your descendants might live" (New Living Translation). Choose life so that you give life to not only you, but your descendants. Choose life so God can reverse the curse and bless you. Choose life so God can grant you a brighter hope and a greater future. Choose life for a cursed blessing can be broken by his blood!

Questions:
1. How would you describe patterns of your family tree in terms of generational blessings and curses?
2. Do you struggle with a particular sin and see a history of it in past generations in your family tree?
3. How do you plan to break the cycle?

Prayer:
Father: "Thank you that generational curses are broken through faith in the blood of Jesus. I put my faith in the blood. I believe Jesus is my mercy seat and that His blood cancels the curse and breaks generational iniquities. I believe, by the blood of Jesus, that the generational curse from the law is canceled and broken off my family now, in Jesus' name. Thank you that sins, bondages and iniquities are canceled and the curse is stopped by the blood of Jesus. Thank you, God, that the blood of Jesus on the mercy seat is a barrier and that a curse cannot pass the blood. Amen." (Walking by Faith: Breaking Generational Curses, Duane Vander Klok).

GOD BLESS YOU

Matthew 5:3

Day 40

Matthew 5:3, *New Living Translation*

- *God blesses those who...*

The renowned and often-quoted song "God Bless America" was a patriotic song written by a man named Irving Berlin during World War I (1918). The song, however popular, is often misquoted or quoted out of context as it was revised twenty years later. As the political and social climate grew more intense in America, Irving revised the song, writing a new stanza in the form of a prayer. Its revised opening lines begin, "While the storm clouds gather / Far across the sea, / Let us swear allegiance / To a land that's free. / Let us all be grateful / For a land so fair, / As we raise our voices./ In a solemn prayer" (Irving). Because of this new edition, "God Bless America" became America`s calling card, acting as a short prayer of prosperity for the nation. A similar phrase is also quoted upon hearing one sneeze. In this case, it is said that people once believed a sneeze caused someone to expel their soul, so "God bless you" was used as a means of protection from the devil snatching your soul. Other origins state that during the bubonic plague, a fatal disease, people would often say "God bless you" as a prayer of protection during such an unprecedented time. When was the last time someone told you or you told someone "God bless you" *not* in context of a sneeze, but just a genuine, heart-felt "God bless you?"

The Gospel according to Matthew is the first book of the New Testament. Authorship is attributed to Matthew, a tax collector who recounts the life, death, and resurrection of Jesus. The book begins teaching us of the messianic lineage of Jesus as we learn he will deliver the people from slavery, provide new teaching (contrary to that of the Israelite leaders), save individuals from sin, and initiate a new covenant with the people for Jesus is God wrapped in the flesh of humanity. Jesus begins his Sermon on the Mount, a series of teachings intended directly to his disciples but ultimately to all of the world past and present. The Israelite leaders saw Jesus as a threat, so they plotted and conspired against him, while Jesus formed his own committee of 12 disciples, or followers whose purpose was to spread and teach the Gospel. One of his disciples, Judas, betrays Jesus as Jesus is falsely arrested, put on trial, rejected as the Messiah, sentenced to death, but later resurrected to continue his mission. The first sermon attributed to Jesus on the Mount is referred to as the Beatitudes, eight blessings declared by Jesus, serving as affirmations. "God blesses those: who are poor and realize their need for him, those who mourn, those who are humble, those who hunger and thirst for justice, those who are merciful, those whose hearts are pure, those who work for peace, and those who are persecuted for doing right" (Matthew 5, New Living Translation).

I was a very insightful young man and one of the biggest questions I had growing up was, "Why do good things happen to bad people?" and I did not realize the answer until now: because they're doing *something* right. The Beatitudes of Jesus are generic and common and I believe it is so Jesus can justly bless everyone, equivalizing this to a participation prize. What human doesn't meet one of the requirements for blessings according to Jesus? There is someone somewhere who is poor, who mourns at least once in their lifetime, who is humble at least in one aspect of life, who hungers and thirsts for justice at least once in a lifetime, who has a pure heart, who works for peace of mind, self, or others, or even one who is persecuted or punished even when doing the right thing. Reflect on your life. How many of the Beatitudes do you fulfill? The more, the merrier. Even on the worst of days, God blesses you. When we have a bad day we like to think we are not blessed, but you`re blessed just to have a brain to think with, feet to walk with, a tongue to talk with. You`re blessed to have a job you may not even like; you're blessed every time you inhale and exhale; you`re blessed with vision, with sight, with smell, with touch, with taste. Count your blessings for they are everywhere. Honestly, if you had a bag filled with all your blessings, the bag would be so overfilled that there would be no evidence of a bag itself for you are blessed. Even more interesting, is that affirmations of blessings extend beyond the Beatitudes. Read the book of Psalms for David gives several more blessings on your behalf. You *are* blessed. Never think otherwise. GOD. BLESS. YOU.

Questions:

1. How many of the Beatitudes do you fulfill?
2. How do you know you are blessed?
3. Major blessings aside, what small blessings have you received today?
4. How can you be a blessing to someone today? Tomorrow? Every day?

Prayer:

Father: I thank you for it all: the good, the bad, the great, the small. Help me to seek your blessings daily because you keep on blessing me. Forgive me for not acknowledging them all. Father, I ask while you bless me, help me to be a blessing to others even if it is as simple as a genuine "God bless you." Bless me as I bless you. In Jesus` name I pray. Amen.

HOMEGROWN

Mark 4:14 ; Mark 6:4

Day 41

Mark 4: 14, *New Living Translation*
- *The farmer plants seed by taking God's word to others.*

Mark 6:4, *God's Word Translation*
- *But Jesus told them, "The only place a prophet isn't honored is in his hometown, among his relatives, and in his own house."*

The germination of seeds is a tedious, yet rewarding process. The first step is selecting your seed. It is noted that the easiest plants to grow from seed are those with larger seeds, while smaller seeds are more difficult (MasterClass). Secondly, one must choose a container. Rather than sowing seed directly in an outdoor garden—where birds and any number of critters may eat them—consider sowing them indoors to ensure safety (MasterClass). Next, plant your seeds, ensuring you water and care for them daily. As seeds begin to germinate, they need to be hardened, referring to the process where indoor seedlings are gradually exposed to outdoor conditions (colder temperatures, wind, direct sunlight). As the weather becomes more ideal, take your "home grown" seeds and transplant them outdoors without damaging its roots allowing them to properly break into its new soil (MasterClass). Where does your seed lie? Notice that seeds must first be home grown before being transplanted. Oftentimes we get so comfortable living in our "home grown" state that we fail to branch out or transplant ourselves due to comfortability and fear. But just like the seed that begins at home, it is imperative that you transplant yourselves for an optimal and even greater impact. Despite your seed being home-grown, you can transplant yourselves elsewhere; but be careful not to damage your roots tied to your "homegrown-ness." Never forget where you came from.

In the book of Mark, people are still enthralled by Jesus` revolutionary character as he performs miracles and forgives individuals, claiming his role as the Messiah. Because of the nature of his character, some follow Jesus, some reject him, and some do not know what to believe. Even the disciples struggled to understand the complexity of his character as they view Jesus as their leader to fame and fortune and not to saving souls who are lost. In Mark 4, Jesus gives a parable about spreading God's word and the impact it has on one's life. Jesus mentions four types of seeds and he defines them by location: a footpath, rocky soil, embedded in thorns, and good soil. Each seed has its own purpose and meaning. The footpath seed represents those who hear God's message, but allows the Devil to take it away during trying times; in other words, allowing the Devil to cause you to falter in faith. The seed in rocky soil represents those who hear the message and are immediately filled with joy, but since their roots are not deep, their joy does not last long and they fall away as soon as problems arise or people criticize or challenge their faith. The seed in thorns represents those who hear God's word, but lose the essence of it due to material desires over spiritual ones, so no fruit is produced. Lastly, the seed in good soil represents those who hear and accept God's word and produce a plentiful harvest. Where does your seed lie? What does the location of your seed say about your character and those who you need to reach?

In Mark 6:4, Jesus returns home to Nazareth to teach and spread the Gospel. People questioned his ability, his integrity, his power. Jesus responded to the people, "The only place a prophet isn't honored is in his hometown, among his relatives, and in his own house" (Mark 6:4, God's Word Translation). Jesus is illustrating that although you may be home grown, not in all cases do the people of your home honor, respect, value, or accept what God has called you to. Sometimes, you have to leave home to fulfill your calling and to spread God's word. Yes, home. Home: a place of comfortability. Home: a place of familiarity. Home: a place of peace and satisfaction. Home: a crutch to hinder one`s calling. I once read a quote that stated, "A [soda] costs $1.00 in a vending machine, $2.00 in a grocery store, and between $3.00 and $5.00 at a theme park. The only thing that changed is its location. The next time you do not feel like you don't have any worth, consider maybe that it is not you; maybe it's your location. Finding the place God intends for you to be, will change everything" (Anonymous). Mark 4:14 states to *take* God's word to others, not stay home and catch those who visit, stop by, walk by, swing by, or you see daily. Merriam-Webster defines "take" as "to lead, carry, or cause to go along to another place." While you may be grown at home, just like the seed, you may need to plant yourself elsewhere to fulfill your calling. Just as a germinating seed has to be transplanted outdoors to be hardened, symbolically speaking, leaving home often makes you harder, stronger, greater, better. Before you begin your "taking", reflect on your making, asking yourself where your seed lies: a footpath, rocky soil, embedded in thorns, or on good soil? And once you can confidently affirm you are home grown on good soil, step out on faith to fulfill your calling so you can be and receive all God intends for you.

Questions:
1. Where lies your seed?
2. What is your calling?
3. What`s your worth?

Prayer:
Father: Transplant me in good soil. I, too, have had instances where I have been planted on footpaths, planted in rocky soil, and planted in thorns. Help me to use my homegrown character to reach those outside of my comfort zone, outside of my homeland. Give me the heart to leap out on faith for you did not give me the spirit of fear, but power, love, and a sound mind. In Jesus` name I pray. Amen.

FEND OFF THE FIEND

Luke 4:4

Day 42

Luke 4: 4, *New Living Translation*

- *"The Scriptures say..."*

In July 2007, a Japan publishing company called SCRAP created the first modern escape room. An escape room is a real-life simulation of a video game in which multiple players are locked in a room with one mission: escape. There are a series of timed tests and challenges groups must pass to escape, often related to pattern recognition, word games, riddles, or puzzles (logic, math, physical). Escape rooms come in a variety of themes and they serve as an entertaining way to build logic and critical thinking in an engaging and entertaining manner. Escape rooms have become more and more popular, expanding to over 60 countries worldwide. They draw inspiration from various traditional games such as Live Action Role Playing, or LARPing (where individuals role-play characters from games or people from past events), scavenger or treasure hunts, and even interactive events such as haunted houses. If not solved, the moderator will unlock the room and give you the answers to the challenges. Although these rooms are created for a fictional and fun experience, when life traps us in real rooms with seemingly no way to escape, how do we respond when the "exit" is not provided if we don't manage to solve it? While there are many types of "escape rooms" the devil traps us in, I`d like to expound on escape rooms of temptations so that we can fend off the fiend.

The book of Luke is part one of a two volume work: Luke/Acts. Luke`s purpose is to show how Jesus is the fulfillment of God and the world. The book begins with the parallel births of John the Baptist and Jesus. While John is the prophetic messenger who will prepare Israel to meet their God, Jesus is the Messianic king who will bring God's reign and blessings. As we learned in Mark`s devotional, Jesus returned to Nazareth and it is here he is welcomed by the Devil, an old fiend. Jesus had just finished a forty day fast as the Devil tempted him each day. Three of the temptations are highlighted in Luke 4. The Devil asks Jesus, "If you are the Son of God, tell the stone to become a loaf of bread" (Luke 4:3, New Living Translation). It is said that the quickest way to a man's heart is through his stomach and the Devil knew this because the devil succeeded in tempting the first sinless man with fruit (Adam) and so he tried to use that attempt on the second sinless man (Jesus), to no avail. Jesus responded, "No! The Scriptures say, People do not live on bread alone" (Luke 4:4, New Living Translation). The Devil tried to up the ante. He took Jesus to a mountain that overlooked all the kingdoms, tempting, "I will give it all to you if you worship me" (Luke 4:7, New Living Translation). The Devil knew Jesus existed to win back the world but wanted to offer an "out" by not having to die on the cross. Jesus replied, "The Scriptures say, You must worship the Lord your God and serve only him" (Luke 4:8, New Living Translation). The Devil tried one more scheme as he took Jesus to Jerusalem to the top of the Temple and commanded, "jump off!" The Devil tried to throw God's word at Jesus for justification arguing, "For the Scriptures say, he will order his angels to protect and guard you...they will hold you up with their hands so you won't even hurt your foot on a stone" (Luke 4:11, New Living Translation). Jesus retorted, "The Scriptures also say, you must not test the Lord your God" (Luke 4:12, New Living Translation). At this, the bible writes "he [the Devil] left him."

How do you fend off the fiend when there is no exit sign in sight? How do you fend off the fiend when you're in the middle of an escape room test? How do you fend off the fiend when he seems to follow you wherever you go as if he's on your security detail? How do you fend off the fiend when he tempts you with good when God will give you greater if you just remain faithful and fight the Devil off? Jesus gives us the answer in Luke 4: talk back to the Devil. How? By using the Word of God. You don't have to try to formulate your own response for God has given you all the words you need in *his* Word. For every temptation the Devil offered, Jesus responded with a Word from God stating "For the Scripture says...". Talk back to the Devil using God's Word. The Devil tried to get slick on his last attempt as he tried to use Scripture (for even the Devil knows and can quote Scripture), but Jesus responded to Satan`s misuse of Scripture with its proper use as God intended and with that, the Devil had no option but to flee. The bible says in 1 Corinthians 10:13, "The temptations in your life are no different from what others experience. And God is faithful. He will not allow the temptation to be more than you can stand. When you are tempted, he will show you a way out so that you can endure (New Living Translation)." *His* words have power. Use the authority that God has given you to make the Devil flee for the Word of God is the answer to fend off the fiend.

Questions:

1. How do you fend off the fiend? Why this approach?
2. What Scriptures can you put in your arsenal to fend off the fiend's attacks?

Prayer:

Father: I thank you for your Word. Further, I thank you for providing a way of escape for every temptation of the Devil. Help me to study to show myself approved to fend off any attack by the fiend. Grant me Godly wisdom, knowledge, and understanding. This I ask in Jesus` name. Amen.

ENDLESS POSSIBILITIES

John 21:25

Day 43

John 21:25, *New International Version*

- *Jesus did many other things as well. If every one of them were written down, I suppose that even the whole world would not have room for the books that would be written.*

In 1974 Erno Rubik, a professor who studied sculpture and architecture, invented the 3 by 3 Rubik's cube—one of the most outstanding, yet perplexing objects due to its simplistic build, yet challenging task. While all Rubik's cubes come pre-solved, the goal is to shuffle the configuration so that each side is a single color or pattern. Solving a Rubik's cube helps to improve performance in analogous tasks, reasoning, logic, and hand-eye coordination. Though so simple, a Rubik's cube offers endless possibilities in solving it as no two people would shuffle nor solve the cube exactly the same. There are over 43 quintillion combinations for a Rubik's cube, though it is possible to always solve one in 20 moves or under. Because quintillions are unfathomable to most calculators, it is even more unfathomable and even impossible for a human being to solve every combination to a Rubik's cube in a single lifetime because its possibilities are endless.

John`s Gospel is attributed to either John the Elder or John of Zebedee, with its purpose of encouraging belief that Jesus is the Messiah. As Jesus traveled, taught his disciples, and performed miracles, signs, and wonders, growing opposition ensued amongst the religious leaders for challenging their teaching and their worldviews. John`s Gospel details Jesus` journey and the people he encounter who give their understanding of who Jesus is followed by Jesus telling him who he truly is: bread of life, light of the world, door of the sheep, good shepherd, resurrection and the life, the way, the truth, and the life, and the true vine. As Jesus journeys, he performs several miracles, signs, and wonders, most notably turning water into wine at a wedding, healing the son of an Official, healing a paralytic man at a pool, walking on water, feeding 5,000 people from two fish and five loaves of bread, healing a man born blind, and even raising Lazarus from the dead. While these seven acts are specifically mentioned in the book of John, Jesus performed several other miracles outside of John's gospel. The book ends "Jesus did many other things as well. If every one of them were written down, I suppose that even the whole world would not have room for the books that would be written" (John 21:25, New International Version). John is teaching that if he wrote down *all* the miracles Jesus performed, the world could not contain it all. John did not say a bookshelf, a library, a skyscraper; he said the world. Can you imagine that? The possibilities of Jesus are endless. Just because it's not in the bible, doesn't mean Jesus didn't do it, can`t do it, nor will do it because in all likelihood he did it before and can surely do it again.

John teaches us in the opening lines of the book, "In the beginning was the Word, and the Word was with God, and the Word was God" (John 1:1, New International Version). If the two are equated, then what we find in the bible *is* a true representation of God: every miracle, every sign, every wonder; his thoughts, his action, his words; his burial, his resurrection, his life. Because God and the Word are synonymous, we must look to it for insight, for guidance, for direction. Because no person`s life is exactly like another, we may look in the Bible and think to ourselves that our story isn't in there; the miracle we need isn`t in there; the answer we need isn`t in there but I came to tell you that it doesn't need to be for God`s possibilities are endless. John writes, "Jesus did many other things as well. If every one of them were written down, I suppose that even the whole world would not have room for the books that would be written" (John 21:25, New International Version). Just like a Rubick`s cube is built with endless possibilities, so are the miraculous powers of God. The bible teaches, "For we do not have a high priest who is unable to empathize with our weaknesses..." (Hebrews 4:15, New International Version). Every trial, every test, every temptation—Jesus has endured. Just because your story isn't written does not mean it does not exist because with Jesus, the possibilities are endless.

Questions:

1. What are you praying to God to do in your life? Do you believe he can? Do you believe he will?
2. Do you pray believing that Jesus` possibilities are restricted or endless? Why?
3. Do you put limitations on your prayers? Why?

Prayer:

Father: Thank you for being a God full of wonder and endless possibilities. Father in your word you declare that "with you all things are possible." Help me to never put restrictions on your purpose, your power, and my prayers. In Jesus` name I pray. Amen.

YOU`RE IN GOOD HANDS

Acts of the Apostles 28:3 ; Acts of the Apostles 28:8

Day 44

Acts of the Apostles 28:3; 28:8, *New Living Translation*
- *3: As Paul gathered an armful of sticks and was laying them on the fire, a poisonous snake, driven out by the heat, bit him on the hand.*
- *8: As it happened, Publius's father was ill with fever and dysentery. Paul went in and prayed for him, and laying his hands on him, he healed him.*

In 1942 there was a man named Davis Ellis who was just hired as the Educational Director at Allstate Insurance Company. His job was to recruit and train female agents. Over the years he became the company's Senior Vice President of Sales, offering one of the greatest contributions to the Allstate company, even known today. Eight years later, Ellis` daughter JoAnn, an honor student and valedictorian of her graduating class, suffered from hepatitis. The family physician, Dr. Cummings advised Ellis that JoAnn was very sick, but he would call in a specialist named Dr. Keyser who may be able to offer greater insight on the medical matter of JoAnn. That evening as Ellis returned from his job at Allstate, his wife Helen rushed to him, threw her hands around him and said, "Dave, the specialist has examined JoAnn and Dr. Cummings tells me that JoAnn is in good hands with Dr. Keyser." JoAnn later recovered, proving she was indeed in good hands. Later that year, Ellis was charged with working on the company's ad campaign as they suggested slogan after slogan, not seeming to find the right fit. Ellis suddenly remembered the words of Dr. Cummings, remembering the level of comfort and ease of anxiety he felt when learning his daughter would be "in good hands." Ellis suggested the slogan, "you're in good hands" as Allstate adopted the phrase immediately. Since 1950, the slogan has become the hallmark of the Allstate brand. Not only was JoAnn in good hands with Dr. Keyser, but she was in even greater hands in that of the Lord`s because spiritually speaking, Jesus is the only insurance that you need.

The book of Acts is the second installment in the Luke/Acts duology with a purpose of showing Jesus` actions and teaching. As Jesus continues to instruct his disciples about life in the kingdom, he encourages them to spread the Gospel to other nations so people would live under his reign. Later in the book, the disciples experience their first encounter with the Holy Spirit (Pentecost). As Jesus became more and more popular, he needed more religious leaders. One leader named Stephen gets arrested for this association as he exposes the truth of the Israelite leaders. He is later murdered, to which Jesus and his disciples are sent out from Jerusalem to proclaim the kingdom of God, expanding internationally. Near the end of the book, Paul is accused and arrested, giving Paul time to write letters to various churches as his form of ministry to spread the Gospel. In the 27th and 28th chapter, the bible shows that Paul had three types of insurance, defined as protection against an eventuality: life, travel (ship), and home. In the 27th chapter, Paul and his men experience a shipwreck so they have to swim to shore; but in the 28th chapter the Lord provides them a new ship to continue the journey, showing he had the Lord's travel insurance to which he did not even have to pay a deductible.

Secondly, in the 28th chapter, as Paul was attempting to build a fire, he reached for some sticks and was bit on the hand by a poisonous snake. The bible writes, "But Paul shook off the [poisonous] snake into the fire and was unharmed" (Acts of the Apostles 28:5, New Living Translation). It did not swell, nor did Paul die, showing Paul had the Lord's life insurance policy. Thirdly, Paul and his men had the Lord's home insurance as they came to a home owned by Publius, the chief of the island. Being a chief, the home must have been heavily guarded and protected, as again, Paul must have had the Lord's home or lodging insurance policy. What is even more revelatory is that while there, Publius` father was ill so the bible writes "Paul went in and prayed for him, and laying his hands on him, he healed him" (Acts of the Apostles 28:8). Notice the same hand that the snake bit that did not harm Paul, was the same hands Paul used for healing a sick man. The lesson here is that the tactics people use to hurt our hands, Jesus uses those hands—our hands—to help others, just as Paul did. Just as Paul was in good hands, we too, are in good hands for Jesus is the only spiritual insurance that we need.

Statistics show that the most popular insurance policies humans hold are life, auto/travel, and home. In these two chapters we see that Jesus offers Paul all three without a single cost paid. Scripture teaches us that Jesus` insurance policy is free. There are no payments, no deductible, no interest charge, no annual change in policy, sign-up charge, and even no hidden fees for it is all laid out in the book of life. You just have to be willing to "give up your own way, take up your cross, and follow [Jesus]" (Matthew 16: 24, New Living Translation). Give it all to God. Hold nothing back. Let him insure your heart, your home, your health, your wealth, your career, your cares, your car, your kids, your relationships, your family, your friends, your faith. God is all the spiritual insurance that you need. Trust and believe you`re in good hands. He made us with his hands, made our home in his hands, and will uplift us with his hands even when life tries to knock us down. Take refuge in the hands of the Father. We are in good hands. Statefarm, Allstate, Progressive, Nationwide, Liberty Mutual, Geico, Travelers, Prudential, USAA, Blue Cross, and any other you can name offers you any insurance policy under the sun, but they all lack insurance for the Son that truly matters—the Son of God. "[Jesus] is the way, the truth, and the life. No man comes to the Father except through [him]" (John 14:6, New International Version), proving the only way to salvation is through Jesus` insurance policy. You`re in good hands.

Questions:
1. Do you feel you are "in good hands?" What makes you feel this way?
2. In what ways has God shown his insurance in your life i.e. your protection from harm and danger, both seen and unseen?
3. How can you increase your faith and trust through Jesus` insurance policy?

Prayer:
Father: You are all the spiritual insurance that I need. Your policy is full of grace, of guidance, of protection, of peace, of joy, and most importantly of love. I realize sometimes I put more trust in man-made policies than I do in yours. Forgive me. I sign on the dotted line and submit to your policy fully. I am all in. In Jesus` name I pray. Amen.

ACCEPT, NOT EXCEPT

Romans 15:17

Day 45

Romans 15:7, *New Living Translation*

- *Therefore, accept each other just as Christ has accepted you so that God will be given the glory.*

In Shakespeare's play *The Merchant of Venice* we are introduced to a Jewish man named Shylock who is socially unaccepted and ostracized due to his race and practice. At this time in history, Jews were treated harshly and unfairly by Christians. Since Christians could not lend money and Jews could, Christians resented Jews for making money off of somebody`s financial need. In the context of the play, Shylock is a usurer or a money-lender who charges extremely high interest rates on loans. The play is centered on a man named Antonio, a Venetian merchant, who is in need of money to help his best friend Bassanio court a woman named Portia, a wealthy heiress. Because of their past grudges, Shylock is at first hesitant to loan the money to Antonio, but after some persuading and manipulating Shylock agrees he will lend Bassanio 3,000 ducats with no interest; but if the loan goes unpaid, Shylock will be entitled to a pound of Antonio's flesh. In one of the play`s most renowned speeches, Shylock appeals to the emotions of the Venetians as he shares the effects of him being outcast and not accepted in society. Shylock states, "I am a Jew. Hath not a Jew eyes? Hath not a Jew hands, organs, dimensions, senses, affections, passions; fed with the same food, hurt with the same weapons, subject to the same diseases, healed by the same means, warmed and cooled by the same winter and summer as a Christian is? If you prick us do we not bleed? If you tickle us do we not laugh? If you poison us, do we not die? And if you wrong us shall we not revenge? If we are like you in the rest, we will resemble you in that" (3.1.49-61). Shylock's speech can be summarized in one statement: acceptance, not "except-ance" (exclusion).

The book of Romans offers a similar message of acceptance—the idea of not excluding one due to their race, religion, sexual orientation, interests, education, customs, culture and others. The book is authored by Paul, formerly known as Saul who had a radical encounter with Jesus, making him an apostle. Paul is known for forming churches and writing letters to said churches to spread the good news of Jesus Christ. Though Jews were once expelled under the reign of Roman Emperor Claudius, they—along with the Jesus-following Jews—were allowed to return to Rome; when they did, the Jews found a church that was very non-Jewish in customs and practices, bridging a divide and tension amongst the Jewish and non-Jewish people. Paul, then, wrote this letter to unify the divided church to teach how to accept and not "except" anyone no matter Jew or Gentile: These—and other such commandments—are summed up in this one commandment: "Love your neighbor as yourself." Love does no wrong to others, so love fulfills the requirements of God's law" (Romans 13:10, New Living

Translation). Love as he loves us. Paul gives four steps to accept people through love: don`t judge others (14:12), don't harm others (14:15), be considerate (15:1), and build others up (15:2). Paul teaches us not to judge for God is the only judge of our character, for it is his and only his judgment for us that matters. His judgment yields life or death, while our judgment speaks only of death on ourselves and the people we judge. Secondly, we can't harm others to please ourselves. Whether intentionally or unintentionally, if through our actions, words, or deeds we bring harm to others, we have to change. We have to accept people for who they are and realize the only thing we can change is ourselves. Thirdly, we must be considerate. The only person on this planet like you is you and you must realize differences exist on a macro and micro scale. We have to be considerate of others` worldview, beliefs, mindset, perspective, and character for we are all God's children—uniquely and wonderfully made. Lastly, we must build others up. Each one, teach one. Don't possess the crab mentality of pulling each other down when one crab tries to do better and rise above their circumstance; instead lift each other up and succeed as one.

Whether we choose to accept it or not, we all have biases against people whether we think of them, act on them, or even promote them. What is important is that we love each other as Christ loves us. While Paul provides direction on accepting others, we first have to accept ourselves as we truly are. We must do a self-inventory on our own identity before we can accept others. Jesus accepts you; why can't we accept ourselves? Accept others? Revelation 7:9 writes, "After this I saw a vast crowd, too great to count, from every nation and tribe and people and language, standing in front of the throne and before the Lamb" (New Living Translation). If God does not discriminate against who can and cannot get in heaven, why do we believe we have the audacity to discriminate, be prejudiced, or even look down on others? Challenge yourself each day to find ways to accept yourself and others, and not "except" for just as we want to be accepted by God we need to accept ourselves and all those whom we encounter.

Questions:

1. Do you accept your total self? Why or why not?
2. How can you accept your total self?
3. To whom do you not accept i.e discriminate against, ostracize, condescend etc? Why? (Be honest with yourself).
4. How can you be more accepting and less "except-ing?"

Prayer:

Father: Strengthen me to accept others and myself as you have already accepted me. I ask that you reveal and rid any biases, hate, prejudice, and discriminatory thoughts, acts, and beliefs I have for anyone other than myself. Help me to spread love just as you love me. In Jesus` name I pray. Amen.

ORDER OF SERVICE

1 Corinthians 14:33

Day 46

1 Corinthians 14:33, *Contemporary English Version*

- *God wants everything to be done peacefully and in order. When God's people meet in church...*

Amidst a court case, a judge bangs the gavel, asserting "order...order in the courtroom!" We see this assertive command and compelling action demonstrated in court cases frequently, whether in reality or as seen on television. The command "order" is shouted when a member or members present in a courtroom have said or acted in a way deemed disruptive or inappropriate i.e. talking out of turn, interrupting the judge, plaintiff, defendant, or witness, or engaging in argumentative behavior. The command "order" encourages members present in the courtroom to desist from intrusive or obtrusive behavior, to behave themselves, and to silence and govern oneself accordingly. Similarly, it is like calling a platoon to "attention", a parent signaling a child by raising their hand, encouraging them to cease talking, or by a coach blowing a whistle. Within a classroom setting, teachers may use a call and response (a common example is when the teacher says "1, 2, 3, eyes on me" and the students reply "1, 2, eyes on you"), clap out a particular rhythm, or perform a countdown. Whatever the action or command, the intended result is to produce order—"the state of peace, freedom from unruly behavior, and respect for law or authority" (Merriam-Webster). In a church setting, when a pastor or clergy shouts or asserts the word "Amen", may be the closest tactic to establishing order, however Paul teaches that as much as we *want* church to be disorderly, order must be established for understanding and for purpose.

Corinth: a major port city with a big economic center is the addressee of this letter by Paul. Although Paul spent over a year at Corinth, when he left, he received word that things were not going well, prompting him to write this letter to rectify five main issues: divisions in the church, sex, food (sacrifices), weekly worship protocol, and perceptions of Jesus` resurrection. While all five issues are relevant, the focus of this devotion is weekly worship protocol. Within the church at Corinth, many people were adept in speaking in tongues, giving testimonies, singing, prophesying, teaching, and interpreting revelation. The issue the people of Corinth faced is that they had no order in doing these things. Because everyone wanted to share and exercise their Godly gifts and abilities, it became distracting as people lost focus on the true meaning of gathering: to glorify Jesus Christ. It could almost be equated to a chaotic classroom: one group of kids gossiping, a few walking around, a few arguing with one another, another few sleeping, a handful playing a collaborative game on their devices, and then two faithful ones trying to listen and learn. While all members are functioning (just like members of a church), the two who recognize the purpose of education suffer at the expense of those who do not care and only wish to practice their selfish and inconsiderate ideologies. Paul is teaching to not distract others from receiving and understanding the Gospel while you inconsiderately and flamboyantly exercise your gifts and abilities. He writes, "...everything that is done must strengthen all of you" (1 Corinthians 14:26, New Living Translation).

Imagine church through the lens of an unbeliever in a setting that lacks order. How might they respond? Seeing the flamboyant nature of those who attend church only to seek the attention of others as they speak in tongues, run around, drop and roll on the floor, fall out, or flail their arms and legs might look crazy (terminology of Paul) and turn people off to the Gospel when the one goal is to bring people into the arch of Christ, not scare them away intentionally or even unintentionally. I`m not saying *not* to do these things, but act out of genuinity and not out of flamboyancy, bringing attention to yourself by acting in a manner that is not organically led by the Holy Spirit. What is the purpose of church if we all went just to put on a performance? Save the theatrics for the theater; save your soul for the church. Paul concludes the chapter, "But be sure that everything is done properly and in order" (1 Corinthians 14: 40, New Living Translation). Just as churches follow an order of service, conduct yourselves orderly being led by the Holy Spirit. Exercise your spiritual gifts and abilities with genuinity and purpose to edify God and not yourself or others. Don`t be so selfish to seek so much attention that a soul who needs saving gets lost in your act. Church is for us all, but it is a place of greater purpose for the unbeliever than it is for those who are saved. Act accordingly and not selfishly. I declare order in the church!

Questions:

1. How do you define order in a church setting (looks like, sounds like , feels like etc.)?
2. How can order be practiced within the church setting?
3. In a church setting, why is order helpful? Why is disorder hurtful?

Prayer:

Father: You are a God of order. From the day of creation you have acted in decency and in order. Restore order to the disorderly. For God I realize there are souls that need you that can`t find you due to disorder. Restore order in our churches, our congregations, our communities, our countries, our world. In Jesus` name I pray. Amen.

SUPERHERO

2 Corinthians 11:5

Day 47

---

2 Corinthians 11:5, *New International Version*

- *I do not think I am in the least inferior to those "super-apostles."*

The root word "super" means "over and above; higher in quantity, quality or degree" (Merriam-Webster).

- Superiority: the quality of being at an advantage
- Supersede: take the place of one previously in authority
- Supervisor: a person in charge of a group of people within an organization
- Superintendent: a person who directs or manages an organization, typically a school system

The root "super" has even made its impact on other more specific terms and ideas:

- Super Bowl: football game that is over all others
- Superman: man "over" all others
- Superstar: star "over" all other sports or entertainment stars

     The problem, however, with the root "super" is that it often becomes subjective rather than objective when it comes to the word "superhero." When one ponders the term "superhero", our minds typically takes us to objective qualities such as strength, courage, moral conviction, servitude, supreme intelligence, integrity, altruism, or even driven; however the "superhero" name becomes controversial and subjective when we begin to name superheroes: Superman, Captain America, Hulk, Professor X, Spiderman, Deadpool, The Incredibles, Thanos (yes, Thanos), Reed Richards, Wong, Jesus Christ. The list could be endless. The list could be amended as we all have our own version of what a superhero embodies, represents, looks like, acts like, sounds like, thinks like, and affects others. How would you describe a superhero? Who *qualifies* as a superhero; who does not?

     Paul wrote 2 Corinthians because many people rejected his first letter (1 Corinthians) and rebelled against his authority. Paul, then, decides to visit the church in person, calling it a "painful visit", giving him inspiration to write this letter with "anguish and tears" to show the people of the Church at Corinth of his love and commitment to them and the Gospel. Many rejected Paul as a leader because he was poor, often homeless, earned wages through manual labor, and was always under constant persecution and suffering. Therefore, when the people were exposed to "Super Apostles", they started to think less of Paul. These Super Apostles were wealthy and impressive, which led to the people of Corinth to question Paul's leadership as the "Supers" only cared about promoting themselves and bad-mouthing Paul as an unfit ruler. As Samuel questioned the composition of a true leader or "superhero", 1 Samuel 16: 7 writes, "But the Lord said to Samuel, "Don't judge by his appearance or height, for I have rejected him. The Lord doesn't see things the way you see them. People judge by outward appearance, but the Lord looks at the heart" (New Living Translation). The people of the Corinthian church revered these "Super Apostles" by their outward appearance of wealth, success, prestige, and privilege, yet Paul possessed the true heart of not just a hero, but a superhero. Paul realized the Super Apostles had no comparison to him. Paul and the "Supers" were both avid in biblical reading. While the "Supers" had superior knowledge of Jesus, Paul actually experienced Jesus for himself. While the "Supers" charged a lot for their services, Paul had no desire for money for he earned his own living. While the "Supers" knew not of sacrifice, Paul sacrificed his life for Jesus. While the "Supers" boasted their accomplishments, Paul boasted his weaknesses, recognizing, "I am glad to boast about my weaknesses, so that the power of Christ can work through me. That's why I take pleasure in my weakness, and in the insults, hardships, persecutions, and troubles that I suffer for Christ. For when I am weak, then I am strong" (2 Corinthians 12:9-10, New Living Translation). While the "Supers" looked heroic in physical appearance, Paul possessed the heart of a superhero, though the people could not see it.

The "Supers" wore the title, but Paul wore the heart. The "Supers" had the financial wealth, but Paul held the spiritual wealth. The "Supers" quoted Scripture, while Paul lived Scripture. The "Supers" charged people; Paul changed people. The "Supers" had powers, but Paul had purpose. Who is the real superhero? We often define heroism or even super-heroism in terms of success, wealth, education, materialism, status, prestige, and influence, when the true definition of superheroism was born in a manger. The true definition of superheroism endured hardship and persecution, the true definition of superheroism was rejected, the true definition of superheroism suffered and sacrificed, the true definition of superheroism died on a cross to save a dying world. The true definition of superheroism: Jesus Christ. He is the real MVP. The real GOAT. He is "him." He is a superhero in more ways than one. Having the title of "super" does not equate to a heart of heroism. Having the title of "super" does not equate to a heart of service. Having the title of "super" does not equate to a ticket to heaven for when it is time to be called home, God calls us all one name—"servant." In particular, "Well done, my good and faithful servant" (Matthew 25:21). He does not call us "super", not "manager", not "director", not "chief", not "president", not "Colonel", not "principal", not "foreman", not "pastor", not "bishop", not "governor", not "landlord", not "parent", not "senator", but "servant". Save the title for the real superhero, Jesus Christ.

Questions:
1. What makes Jesus qualified to be a superhero?
2. What acts remind you of his heroism?
3. What words remind you of his heroism?
4. How can you be reminded of his heroism daily?

Prayer:
Father: Thank you for saving me from the greatest enemy of all time: sin. You are the epitome of a superhero and because of that I give you the glory, honor, and praise daily. Your stripes, your suffering, and your saving grace make you an incomparable superhero. Thank you for your service. In Jesus` name I pray. Amen.

I`M GOOD

Galatians 6:9-10

Day 48

Galatians 6: 9-10, *New Living Translation*

- *So let's not get tired of doing what is good. At just the right time we will reap a harvest of blessing if we don't give up. Therefore, whenever we have the opportunity, we should do good to everyone—especially to those in the family of faith.*

When asked "How are you?" Why do people often respond "I'm good" when they really aren't? There could be many answers to this question: one answer could be that the term "good" is subjective. A homeless person who finds shelter in a safe, warm space may be deemed "good" whereas a millionaire may consider possessing shelter for the night as unremarkable or standard. Another reason people typically say they are doing "good" when they really aren't could be because people may not feel like telling the world their story at that moment, thinking no one wants to hear the truth; so we mask our issues by smiling and saying we're "good" because that's the easiest thing to do for us in the moment. Further, the honest answer may make others uncomfortable: "I'm having a colonoscopy done tomorrow and I am anxious" or "I`m having suspicions about my partner and I am concerned" or "I feel like I am losing faith in God" are things that may make another individual wince or simply not know how to respond. Other people decide to answer "good" to not bring down the mood; others may say "good" so they don't have to hear what others have to say or be judged; others say "good" just because they don`t want to talk about it; another may not feel comfortable sharing; another may not be ready to share because they had not dealt with the problem internally—let alone externally; or you may just be one of those individuals who respond "I'm good" out of habit. Whatever the case, the goodness I wish to expound upon is not good in terms of *how* we are, but good in terms of *who* we are.

Paul wrote Galations to members of churches in Galatia in deep passion and frustration. As Jewish Christians moved to Galatian churches, they started undermining Paul and began assimilating all non-Jewish Christians into Jewish customs. This act angered Paul, so he wrote this letter as he wanted to convey that the purpose of the Gospel is not necessarily to observe the laws of the Old Testament, but to save souls to be members of Christ, filling people with love and faith in others and Jesus. In other words, Paul believed the laws had nothing to do with anything; what was truly important was the ultimate sacrifice of Jesus. While Old Testament law exposed Israel's sin, Jesus came and fulfilled the law, encouraging us to never "get tired of doing what is good; whenever we have the opportunity, we should do good to everyone—especially to those in the family of faith." (Galatians 6:9-10); in order to reap a harvest, we first have to plant the fruit. This fruit is summarized in Galatians 5:22: 22-23: love, joy, peace, patience, kindness, goodness, faithfulness, gentleness, and self-control (New Living Translation). In our daily lives our focus is so in tuned with *how* people are and not *who* people are—minding others` business instead of minding about the person *with* the business. I may not be able to help solve your problems, but if I can say or do something good to help you, that may just be what you need to spark that turnaround in your life.

The bible tells us explicitly, "So let's not get tired of doing what is good. At just the right time we will reap a harvest of blessing if we don't give up" (Galatians 6:9, New Living Translation). By being *good* people, we can be good people. In other words, when we are good to people, God will bless us if we don't give up—if we are persistent and consistent in doing good to others. We can`t be good and build each other up on Sunday and be bad and tear each other down throughout the week. God is good all the time; and all the time God is good. Love one another as Christ loves us. Seek and spread joy. Speak peace to you, through you, and around you. Be patient in all circumstances. Be kind to strangers and friends. Be faithful to being good; be faithful to God. Be gentle with others—handle them with care. Practice self-control by refraining from sin and temptation. If we could see what others were facing in their lives just by looking at them, this world would be a much better place. But because God has not gifted us with that ability like he has, we must act as if people are not good; act as if things are not okay; act out of goodness. I challenge you: every single time in a day when someone asks you "how are you"—no matter how you respond—*do* something good for someone. Use each of those opportunities to be good and spread goodness, remembering we serve a *good* God. Declare today: I`m good.

Questions:
1. How are you today?
2. How have you been good to you? How have you been good to others? How has God been good to you?
3. How can you spread goodness today?

Prayer:
Father: I am so glad I know you as a good God. God, you are the epitome of goodness and I ask that you give me the will and commitment to spread goodness wherever I go, realizing that someone I encounter each day needs to be told of your goodness and reminded of the good in them. Help me to encourage others, empower others, and educate others on your goodness and your grace. In Jesus` name I pray. Amen.

GET DRESSED

Ephesians 6:11

Day 49

Ephesians 6:11, *New Living Translation*

- *Put on all of God's armor so that you will be able to stand firm against all strategies of the devil.*

Statistics show that from 1982 to 2015, more than 70,000 officers were assaulted with firearms (Caliber Armor). Even more devastating is that 92% of all felonious deaths of officers in the line of duty were due to firearms (Caliber Armor). There is a vast misconception that only military personnel and government/law enforcement agents wear armor. Armor is described by Merriam-Webster dictionary as a "defensive covering or a protective layer". Essentially, armor serves as protection just as airbags are in cars, mouthguards are worn by athletes, hard hats and steel-toed boots for workers, or gloves and masks for medical professionals. The world is a dangerous place and more and more careers enforce and mandate armor for their employees such as firefighters, EMT`s, private security personnel, bankers, judges, other government officials and—suggested, but not yet (at least) approved for, teachers. People often use armor in recreational activities such as hunting or mountain biking. Wearing body armor offers a greater chance of survival from potentially fatal or injury-prone incidents and offers some people greater confidence, peace, and security going about their daily lives. While knights used to dress in armor of 14 pieces in war, the bible only requires a six-piece uniform to help us "resist the enemy in the time of evil" (Ephesians 6:13, New Living Translation). Get dressed!

The city of Ephesus was a huge city deemed as the epicenter of worship for Greek and Roman gods. Paul stayed there for about two years after his imprisonment by the Romans. Paul begins the letter praising God for the unity of Jew and Gentile through the work of the Holy Spirit. Despite the many titles people may have held (teacher, apostle, pastor, prophet, evangelists etc.) within the church of the time, Paul recognized they are led by one spirit. Paul then teaches the impact of a life in God as God can turn a liar into an honest person, an angry person to a peaceful one, a thief to a generous person, a gossiper to an encourager, a vengeful spirit into a forgiving one etc. Paul closes the letter reminding us of spiritual evils, or beings that seek to undermine or separate us from our union or relationship with Jesus. He describes this as the armor of God—one of the most quoted passages in Ephesians. Paul writes this using the metaphor of a soldier in battle for when the Devil attacks it could be comparable to a warzone. Our uniform consists of six articles, each with their own purpose: a belt of truth, the body armor of God's protection, shoes of peace to stand prepared, a shield of faith to stop the Devil's arrows, a helmet of salvation, and the sword of the Spirit (Word of God). In other words, we need truth, God's protection, peace, faith, salvation, and the Word of God. Get dressed.

War is a game of strategy and skill and the Devil knows and can quote Scripture. Don't be so conceited to think that since you know the Word, you`re exempt from the Devil`s attacks; get dressed. Don`t be so naive to think you have the advantage because you and the Lord go way back; get dressed. Don't think that just because it's too hot that you don't need the full uniform; get dressed. Don`t put your guard down for the Devil to sneak in and claim the victory. The bible teaches us to be "as shrewd as serpents and harmless as doves" (Matthew 10:16, New Living Translation). In other words, have discernment in the Devil's schemes but be harmless in your approach to claim the victory. As you live your lives, dress fully. A soldier in battle needs full armor to win the war: the truth of discernment to guide us, God's divine protection to keep us, a peace that surpasses all understanding to ground us, utmost faith in God to motivate us, salvation in Christ to save us, and the Word of God to educate us. Get dressed! Just as you may suit up in armor for your jobs or careers, the armor of the Lord is much more potent, more powerful, more purposeful, and more protective. His armor never needs washing; his armor will always fit; his armor never rips or tears; his armor never goes out of fashion or style; his armor matches any attire you wear it with; his armor is suitable in any form of weather imaginable; his armor is fitting no matter the event or venue; his armor is all you need to succeed. Get dressed!

Questions:
1. How dressed are you?
2. What article of clothing do you need to wear more often? Why?

Prayer:
Father: Dress me again. I realize that I don`t wear your full armor daily and when I do that, I`m not fully clothed and I become more prone to the Devil`s attacks. Help me to get fully dressed each day and walk in my victory. In Jesus` name I pray. Amen.

JUST DO IT

Philippians 4:13

Day 50

Philippians 4:13, *New King James Version*

- *I can do all things through Christ who strengthens me.*

Gary Gilmore, a double-murderer, killed two people in Utah in 1976. According to U.S Supreme Court records, Gilmore robbed and killed a gas station worker and a motel worker in one evening. Following these killings, while attempting to dispose of the gun, Gilmore shot himself in the hand accidentally and fled to his cousin`s house for medical aid; however his cousin turned him over to the police. Gilmore was sentenced to death in Utah State Prison, choosing to die by firing squad, serving as the first person to be executed in this manner since the Supreme Court struck down the death penalty in 1972. When asked if he had any final words, he responded, "You know; let's do it." This case was highlighted in a documentary called "Art & Copy" by Doug Pray in 2009. Marketing and advertising mastermind, Dan Wieden, known for his marketing campaigns for companies such as Old Spice, Coca Cola, and Proctor and Gamble, drew inspiration from this incident, creating the tagline for Nike: "Just Do It." This phrase catapulted Wieden`s already successful career as Nike debuted the slogan in a 1988 commercial, keeping the tagline as a part of their brand. The phrase is quoted regularly to inspire and motivate individuals to not just purchase Nike products, but to chase their wildest dreams and endeavors. Just do it!

The church in Philippi was the first church Paul started in eastern Europe. It was a retirement community, known for its patriotism and nationalism. As Paul continued his mission of proclaiming the Gospel, the followers he left there also faced persecution and resistance. While imprisoned, however, the Philippians sent a man named Epaphroditus with a financial gift to Paul. Paul wrote this letter as a means of expressing gratitude for the gift. Paul begins the letter with a prayer of gratefulness, giving thanks to God for the generosity and faithfulness of the Philippians. Though in prison, Paul recognized the advancement of the Gospel as more and more people became open and confident about sharing God's Word. It is there, in prison, where Paul had an epiphany: dying would be a gain. If he were to die, he would be present with the Lord; if he lives, it gives him greater opportunity to spread the Gospel and start more churches. Paul`s purpose was to show that Jesus is a way of life that should be imitated by putting others before ourselves by serving and loving others. Paul closes the letter, thanking and urging the church of Philippi "not to worry about anything, but pray about everything" (Philippians 4:6, New Living Translation) as Paul realized his hardships were his greatest teachers, quoting: "I can do all things through Christ who strengthens me" (Philippians 4:13, New King James Version). Just do it.

Scripture reminds us constantly that God is the source of our strength. Isaiah 40: 29 states, "He gives power to the weak and strength to the powerless" (New Living Translation). If God is the source of our strength, why do we have doubts or second, third, and even fourth thoughts about walking in our purpose; for if we rely on the Lord's strength, failure will not be our future, success will. How do we know the potency of our purpose if we do not first try? Living in an "Alexa" world has many of our minds misconstrued, thinking that when we ask God for something, he`ll give and we`ll get the answer immediately, like Alexa or Siri. But if that is the case, what is the purpose of faith? The bible says, "faith is the substance of things hoped for, the evidence of things not seen" (Hebrews 11:1, King James Version). The bible does not say "faith is the substance of things asked for, the evidence of what is seen" for if we ask it and receive it immediately, faith has no function. With a willing spirit and the source of the Lord, you can do anything. Just do it. My question to you is, if your ideas could speak, what would they say to you? What ideas have you been sitting on wanting to do, but have not yet begun? Write a book? Just do it. Start a business? Just do it. Apply for a job? Just do it. Start that savings or joint savings account? Just do it. Buy that home? Just do it. Shoot your shot for that relationship? Just do it. Go back to school? Just do it. Volunteer in the community? Just do it. Lead that committee? Just do it. Serve in the church? Just do it. Get that passport? Just do it. Take that vacation? Just do it. Everything and anything you didn't think possible or even doubted, just do it! Checkmarks are used for two reasons: to signify a "good job" on an assignment *or* to signify something is complete when checking off a to-do list or grocery list. Although Nike`s check symbolizes motion and speed, I declare and decree that every checkmark you see is confirmation that your dream is already done. Step out on faith. Just do it. Be willing to try. Just do it. Be willing to fail. Just do it. Walk into your purpose and your calling. Just do it.

Questions:

1. What is a dream or goal you would complete if you knew you could not fail?
2. What steps can be taken to make that dream or goal become a reality?
3. How can you seek God or his Word for inspiration in fulfilling this dream or goal?

Prayer:

Father: Reveal to me what you already wrote for me. Your word declares that you "know the plans for me: plans to prosper and not harm me, plans to give me a hope and a future." With you I cannot fail. Show me, guide me, and direct me into the future you have for me for what's coming for me is bigger, better, and greater. Grant me the willingness to try and the willingness to persevere just as Paul did through persecution, suffering, and imprisonment. Encourage me to just do it! Thank you in advance. In Jesus` name I pray. Amen.

BROKEN RULES

Colossians 2:20-21

Day 51

Colossians 2:20-21, *Amplified Bible*
- *If you have died with Christ to the elementary principles of the world, why, as if you were still living in the world, do you submit to rules and regulations, such as, "Do not handle [this], do not taste [that], do not [even] touch!"?*

Rules and laws govern life. Everywhere you go has rules, whether written (No soliciting; no littering; no trespassing) or unwritten (be quiet in a library; put the toilet seat down when done; wait for people in an elevator to get off before you enter). As an educator, one must dispel the myth that a classroom must have an extensive list of rules to govern behavior and produce the most disciplined students. My classroom has one rule: respect. Everything you could possibly do or say that is deemed inappropriate, can be satisfied with my one rule: respect. In other words, when it comes to classroom rules, less is more. Less rules = more student accountability. Less rules = more student discipline. Less rules = more likely students will remember and adhere. Less quantity = more quality. If a student breaks a rule, there are often consequences that follow. Think about it: how might a child respond living in a house with too many rules? How might an employee respond to a workplace with too many rules? How might a student respond to a classroom with too many rules? How might a person respond to a bible of too many rules? I recently read an article called "Negative Effects of Too Many Rules on Children" and because rules are universal, these can be applied to not just children, but to all humanity. The author writes having too many rules has two effects on people: it makes people rebel and it makes people confused. Having too many rules can be a turn-off to many. The Israelites were bound to the 600+ laws of the Torah, yet they still rebelled. Our churches are dying today because we preach too many consequences and not enough benefits of a relationship with Jesus. We preach the consequences of sex before marriage; we preach the consequences of stealing; we preach the consequences of disobeying authority, we preach the consequences of alcoholism; and it is this consequence-based approach to religion or this "fear-tactic" that make many youth and young adults leave or fail to see the purpose of church, *not* necessarily religion. Are you ready to hear the truth? Here it is: Just because you follow the rules (e.g commandments), does not guarantee you a one-way, all access pass to heaven. Following the rules does not equal assured salvation.

Paul wrote the letter to the church of Colossae during his imprisonment and it was addressed to people who Paul never met who decided to create a church community, not approved or initiated by Paul. Paul`s purpose was to address cultural pressures that lead people away from Jesus, challenging them to a greater level of devotion to Jesus. One of these cultural pressures was what people , especially Jews, should do with the Torah, a book of 613 laws given by Moses to the Jewish people in the Old Testament. In Colossians, the Jews pressured the non-Jews to follow all the laws of the Torah, but Paul argued to not focus on the laws of the Torah (Old Testament) for two reasons: (1) Jesus` death and resurrection fulfilled the laws of the Torah for he is the reality to which all the laws were appointed and (2) following the rules of the Torah had no effect on the Israelites for abiding by rules does not equate to the mission of Christianity: to transform the heart of people to love and serve others while loving and serving Christ. Following the rules does not mean you are doing the right thing. Just because a student follows all the rules in class, does not mean they`ll pass. Just because you take the medicine prescribed by the doctor, does not mean you won`t die. Just because you cross every "T" and dot every "I", does not mean everyone can read and understand your writing. Just because you pay taxes, does not mean you`ll never be in debt. Just because we follow the Ten Commandments, does not mean we're saved from hell. Since Jesus fulfilled the laws of the Torah, we are free and no longer subject to the laws of the Old Testament. The laws are good, but even the laws did not fix the problem of sin for the Israelites. The solution is Jesus as he released his Spirit to transform us so we can live a new life in him under new law.

The title of this devotional is "broken rules". I am not teaching that because Jesus fulfilled the law that it is justified to break the commandments; what I am teaching is that because Jesus died for our sins and gave us new life and freedom under his reign, the rules are broken, meaning brought to an immediate end. Our churches are dying because we focus so much on the consequence of sin and not enough on the compliments of the Savior. Romans 4:15 writes, "For the law always brings punishment on those who try to obey it. (The only way to avoid breaking the law is to have no law to break" (New Living Translation). Jesus` death provided us freedom, not consequence. If this is the case, why do we preach from the basis of consequence and not the basis of benefits? God gave us ten commandments and simply following them is not enough. You can follow all ten, but if you do not "declare Jesus as Lord and believe in [your] heart that God raised him from the dead" (Romans 10:9, New Living Translation), how can you get into heaven? Paul writes in Colossians 3 that instead of focusing on the consequences of the Old Testament Torah, lend our attention to "tenderhearted mercy, kindness, humility, gentleness, patience, forgiveness, love, peace, thanksgiving, praising" (Colossians 3:12-17) for it is these benefits—not consequences—that secure our seat, our shelter, and our Savior in heaven. You can't break rules that God already broke (brought to an end) for us. Don't be so hard on yourself thinking that because you broke a commandment, you are doomed. Forgive yourself as God has forgiven you. Place your focus on the Godly things you *can* do, and not so much on the commandments you *can`t* do. For the cans outweigh the "can`ts."

Question:
1. How can you shift your focus from the "can`ts" of religion to the "cans" of religion Jesus fulfilled when he died for our sins, giving us new humanity?

Prayer:
Father: Thank you for the freedom we have in Christ. Because we live in his spirit and truth, we have been freed from the constraints of Old Testament law for they, too, were nailed to the cross. Turn my attention from the can`ts of religion so I can focus on the cans your freedom allows. Cans of mercy, kindness, humility, gentleness, patience, forgiveness, love, peace, thanksgiving, and praise. Free at last, free at last; thank God Almighty I am free at last from my past. In Jesus` name I pray. Amen.

F.A.T.H.E.R

1 Thessalonians 2:11

Day 52

---

1 Thessalonians 2:11, *New Living Translation*
- *And you know that we treated each of you as a father treats his own children.*

It is hard being a father in this day and age; it is even harder to be a Black father in this day and age; and it is hardest being a Black, Christain, father in this day and age. Fathers do not have it easy. A Black man in the U.S has an estimated 1 in 1,000 chance of being killed by police—2.5 times the odds for a white man (Journalists Resource). Black men have lower levels of degree attainment than White men in every U.S state; over a quarter of Black men in this day and age hold a college degree at 26.7% (The Education Trust). Black men have the highest unemployment rate for any race and gender group and the lowest labor force participation and employment rate as of 2021 (Brookings). Ask Google what race has the most fatherless children; you`ll find the answer is black children, nearly at 60% (approximately 42 million children), followed by Hispanic (Family Structure and Children's Living Arrangements). Lastly, the biggest issue facing family or social problems today is fatherlessness or lack thereof. Despite setbacks in education, law, parental involvement, job opportunities, and others, Black fathers, in particular, face endless criticism as this population is blamed and considered the scapegoat for many of society's failures. In short, a quote from The San Diego Union-Tribune, states, "If only those Black fathers would get it together they wouldn't see their kids disproportionately punished in schools, they wouldn't see Child Services disproportionately snatch away kids in their communities, they wouldn't see their children gunned down by police because Black kids would know how to respect authority" (Column). Having so many social, economical, physical, educational, and spiritual pressures, along with the many stereotypes people box black fathers in, it is hard to be a father in this day and age; it is even harder to be a Black father in this day and age; it is hardest being a Black, Christian father in this day and age. With so many influences, expectations, stereotypes, criticism, responsibilities, priorities, setbacks, and challenges, and with so little support, so many fathers don't know what to be so they try their best with the cards they've been dealt. Scripture, however, offers insight and direction on being a father as we are introduced to the greatest Father to have ever and will ever live: God, our Father.

The letter addressed to the church at Thessalonica is found to be one of the earliest letters of Paul. Paul and his co-worker Silas went to Thessalonica and after telling them of the Good News, many people gave allegiance to Jesus, causing their persecution for defying Caesar (Roman Emperor) by accepting Jesus. Paul and Silas fled Thessalonica reluctantly so Paul wrote this letter to reconnect with the people after receiving word that they were flourishing, despite persecution. Paul opens the letter thanking God for the allegiance of the people at Thessalonica. In the second chapter, Paul remembers his visit, telling readers of the friendships he formed and reiterating the true purpose of the gospel: forming healthy relationships through love and acts of service. In Thessalonians 2: 10-12, Paul defines what a father should be in six different ways: faultless, assertive, touching, holy, encouraging, righteous or in short: F.A.T.H.E.R.

A father must first be **faultless** or blameless (2:10). In other words, a father must recognize that he has sinned (for we are all subject to sin), yet possess no cause to be accused of wrongdoing in the natural world. A father`s name can`t be in this gossip or in that news or be involved in ungodly character or situations. A father has a name and a family to uphold and a father cannot do that by acting or doing things that could cause the natural world to deem him dishonorable. A father must secondly be **assertive** (2:11). A father must possess bold forcefulness. A father must be able to put his foot down for good cause and his speech must be assertive so it cannot be misconstrued by those who listen. A father must be **touching** ("urging" as used in Scripture; 1 Thessalonians 2:11). A father must have influence by finding ways of touching the hearts and minds of those he encounters. A father must be **holy** (2:10), living lives that are pleasing to God through moral and spiritual excellence. A father must be **encouraging** (2:11), which differs from influence as encouragement shows support. You can influence someone to not drink and drive, but you may not support them by being their designated driver. Encouragement relates to supporting, comforting, and speaking affirmations to those you encounter. Lastly, a father must be **righteous** (2:10), which differs from holiness. Righteousness is the result of holiness. An athlete might be good enough to be in the NBA; righteousness is the athlete`s position in the NBA, but holiness is the athlete`s dedication and devotion to the sport. Holiness is the job description for the title of righteousness. Holiness is being dedicated to moral excellence whereas righteousness is being declared morally excellent. Father: faultless, assertive, touching, holy, encouraging, righteous. Isn't our Father just like this? God meets and exceeds the description of a father according to Scripture. We have to realize that no man is perfect, especially when the odds are against him. Let's not put so much added pressure on our fathers because our fathers are incomparable to *our* Father (capital "F").

Questions:
1. How does your natural father compare to Paul`s definition of a father? How can you support him?
2. (if applicable) How does your spouse (male) compare to Paul`s definition of a father? How can you support him?
3. How does your Father, which art in heaven, compare to Paul`s definition of a father? How can you exalt him?

Prayer:
Father: Thank you for leading by example. Thank you for being a father deemed faultless, a father of assertiveness, a father of influence (touching), a father of holiness, a father of encouragement, a father of righteousness, and a father of so much more. Be a guide of fatherly love and support for our natural fathers so they can learn and live up to your example each and every day. In Jesus` name I pray. Amen.

EARN WHAT YOU EAT

2 Thessalonians 3:10

Day 53

2nd Thessalonians 3:10, *New International Version*
- *For even when we were with you, we gave you this rule: "The one who is unwilling to work shall not eat."*

The most absurd story I once heard from my father was a story he told me about when he was around the age of 18 (circa de 1970). He told me that he and his male siblings, especially, had to work to help provide for his family financially. He recalled one week he had just gotten paid and somehow lost the funds from his paycheck; so when he got home to his parents, he had no money to give them. His punishment? He did not get fed. He told me he had to survive the entire week on snacks (peanut butter crackers), fruit (like watermelon), and drinks such as soda and water because his parents would not let him eat any "real food" if he did not contribute any money to the household for the week. When he first told me of this story, I deemed it laughable or foolish, but he taught me over time that that was the culture of his home and often of the times in which they lived. Similarly, in Zora Neale Hurston's short story called "Sweat", we meet a hardworking, middle-aged black woman who earns her wages washing other people's clothes, named Delia. She is married to a lazy, abusive (physically and emotionally), inconsiderate, and useless man named Sykes, whom the townspeople disdain and mock (justifiably). As Delia is delivering clothes one day, one of the neighborly men say, "[Hot or cold, rain or shine, just as regular as the weeks roll around, Delia carries them and fetches them on Sunday], as she is commended by many by her work ethic to support she and her willingly and contentedly unemployed husband. Another neighbor responds, "She better [work] if she wants to eat" (Hurston). Culturally, the unwritten rule is you must earn what you eat.

In 2nd Thessalonians, Paul received a report that the problems he addressed in the first letter had gotten worse: persecutions intensified and people remained confused about Jesus` return. Paul opens the book with a prayer of endurance, encouraging the Thessalonians not to lose faith in their persecutions and reminding them their suffering comes at the expense of being associated with Jesus as it shows participation in God's kingdom. In chapter 2, Paul addresses confusion around the day of the Lord as people speculated dates, inspiring fear in others. Paul reminds the people of sound teaching regarding the Lord's coming, praying for their comfort and faithfulness to Jesus. In the last chapter, Paul challenges the idle. In this case, the idle did not simply refer to those deemed lazy, but also included those who refused to work. Paul could possibly be referring to the Roman culture tradition of patronage, poor individuals who would act as assistants to the wealthy, living off their occasional generosity (unpredictable means of income). Paul reminds the Thessalonians that he did not ask them for money for his services of his manually laborious job, teaching that followers of Jesus must work to provide for themselves and others to be a benefit to themselves and others. Earn what you eat.

If you are not doing the Lord's will or working in *any* capacity he has intended, for whom or what are you working? For whom or what are you serving? For whom or what are you living? You must earn what you eat. You must work! Yes, unemployment is real; not being able to find and secure a job is real; but the work I am mainly focused on in this devotion is the work of the Lord. The term "work" can be defined in this regards in three ways: "to perform work or fulfill duties regularly for wages or salary" (a job or career), "to keep in motion, operation, or activity", or a "specific task, duty, function, or assignment often being a part or phase of some larger activity" (Merriam-Webster). This "larger activity" is the work of Christ. The bible says "[We] are the salt of the earth. But if the salt loses its saltiness, how can it be made salty again? It is no longer good for anything, except to be thrown out and trampled underfoot" (Matthew 5:13, New International Version). To earn what we eat, we must *be* seasoning. We are called to teach and proclaim God's word; we are called to embody the fruits of the Spirit; we are called to do his work and his will. Don`t do his work for your gain, but his. Don`t do his work for your name, but his. Don`t do his work for your clout, but his. Earn what you eat. Don't be satisfied working just for an appetizer. Work for the side salad. Work for the entree. Work for the main course. Work for the dessert. Work for the beverage. And when *his* work is done, work again for the leftovers, work again for the to-go box, work again for seconds, thirds, and fourths for his work is never done. The bible teaches, "Idle hands are the devil's workshop; idle lips are his mouthpiece" (Proverbs 16: 27, The Living Bible). Hurston's short story concludes with Sykes being bit and killed by a snake. Because Sykes worked for the Devil, he got paid by the Devil, to his demise. Be careful who you pledge allegiance to. Yes, you may have an actual job or career, but just as God allowed you to have it, he can take it away. But, *his* work is a job you can never be fired from. *His* job never downsizes. *His* job never goes bankrupt. *His* job requires no background check, no references, and no experience. No matter the sin, you will always be employed. Earn what you eat and thank God for the food.

Questions:
1. Who do you primarily work for: an employer or the Lord?
2. How many hours per day do you devote to working to benefit yourself and others doing the Lord's work and will?
3. Describe your job description.
4. How does the Lord pay you for your work?

Prayer:
Father: I thank you for my physical and spiritual career. Incline my mind and heart to excel in both careers. Give me direction on how I can be a better worker in both careers, to benefit myself and others, bringing honor and glory to your name. Each week when I get paid, let me be satisfied with my earnings so that I can eat well. In Jesus` name I pray. Amen.

DON`T LEAVE FAITH BEHIND

1 Timothy 4:1

Day 54

---

1 Timothy 4:1, *New International Version*

- *The Spirit clearly says that in later times some will abandon the faith...*

In 1835, Nathaniel Hawthorne published one of his most notable short stories, "Young Goodman Brown." The story is centered around the Salem Witch Trials, a time of hearings and persecutions of people accused of witchcraft in Massachusetts in the late 1690`s as people lived in paranoia, fear, and hysteria. The plot of the text is simple, yet it possesses an allegorical meaning. We meet a man (Goodman Brown) and his wife Faith. As Goodman leaves their home one night, his wife is scared to stay at home alone. He reassures her by telling her to say her prayers, and by doing so, no harm will come upon her. Goodman leaves reluctantly, afraid of the Devil who lurks the woods. He meets a man (deemed the Devil) who tries to entice Goodman, sharing that he knew of Goodman`s father and grandfather and all the immoral deeds they committed. As Goodman attempts to return home, he sees a pious, respected woman named Goody Cloyse, leading Goodman to hide as he is embarrassed to be seen with the man (the Devil), only to find out Goody Cloyse is also a witch. Soon Goodman sees ministers following the Devil, and proclaims, "With Heaven above, and Faith below, I will yet stand firm against the Devil" (Hawthorne). Goodman, then, has hallucinations of seeing and hearing Faith, his father, and other deceased family members. Unbeknownst to Goodman, this was a conversion or an initiation for the Devil to gain followers. The next morning when Goodman woke, he saw the ministers praying, teaching the Bible, and blessing people; Goodman, then, realized the hypocrisy of the religious leaders and was forever changed as he no longer trusts or believes the ministers and no longer loves his wife, Faith. The story concludes, "And when he had lived long, and was borne to his grave, a hoary corpse, followed by Faith, an aged woman, and children and grand-children, a goodly procession, besides neighbors, not a few, they carved no hopeful verse upon his tombstone; for his dying hour was gloom" (Hawthorne). Faith has a dual meaning because although Goodman`s wife`s name is Faith, because he did not carry his faith (in a religious sense) with him, he, his wife, and their lineage were all lost as they died in gloom and not glory. Don`t leave faith behind.

Paul developed many co-workers while church planting; one co-worker`s name is Timothy. Paul mentored and sent Timothy to different churches. After receiving word that the leaders of the church of Ephesus were spreading incorrect views of Jesus, Paul sent Timothy to confront the leaders and restore the church. The leaders were still hung up on the Torah as it divided the church in followers and unfollowers, but Paul corrected this by arguing that correct teaching (the Lord's teaching) leads to gratitude in grace, not division. Paul encouraged the people to hold prayer meetings to pray for their leaders for all issues could be resolved with prayer: anger, pride in materialism, boasting, false teaching, alcoholism, differences and division of the Torah's laws, immoral sexual actions, working for men and not God, dishonor towards men and God etc. 2 Timothy establishes a guide for order in the church in terms of leadership, showing that leaders must be of character and integrity in the home and in the church. While all this is important, what is even more important is why God chose Timothy. The bible says in 2 Timothy 1:5, "I remember your [Timothy] genuine faith, for you share the faith that first filled your grandmother Lois and your mother, Eunice. And I know that same faith continues strong in you" (New International Version). Timothy was chosen because of his faith. Don`t leave faith behind!

Humanity must be more proactive than reactive—more considerate and less selfish. We need to live with an eye on the future. We must live and lead by example, not merely for ourselves, not merely for God, but also for our future. Timothy`s faith was in him, traced back to his mother, and traced back to her mother. Their family established and was grounded in a lineage of faith. Can you say the same for your family? Does faith start with you or stop with you? Yes, being a Christian is a lifestyle, and although it may not be the life you want to lead and live, think about your future...*the* future. If faith stops with you, how might the future be? The world is already chaotic and cold and conniving; imagine if faith stopped with you how much worse the world might be? If you don't teach Jesus to the youth, who will? If you don't take the younger ones to church, who will? Don't leave faith behind. We have to stop making excuses, thinking, waiting, and anticipating for someone else to pick up our slack spiritually. Lead by example. Don't leave faith behind like Goodman did. He left faith and Faith behind and was forever changed. Not only did his actions affect himself, but so did it affect his future generations. "Now faith is the substance of things hoped for, the evidence of things not seen" (Hebrews 11:1, King James Version). The bible uses the word "now", meaning the definition never changes. The time is always now, meaning faith is the same for all past generations, the current one, and all future ones. If faith doesn't change, why do we think our role does? Don`t leave faith behind. Carry it every second, every minute, every hour, every day, every month, every year, every decade, every century, every generation. Don`t leave faith behind!

Questions:
1. What does faith mean to you?
2. How can you possess greater faith?
3. How can you instill and establish faith in your future lineage to establish generational faith?

Prayer:
Father: Give me the faith I need not merely to exist, but to live and reap every benefit of you. I realize that with faith, I am pleasing in your sight. I pray that when you look at me when I am on the hill or low in a valley, when I have no makeup or have a bad hair day, when I am tired and weak, that you always see me the same: with pleasure. Because you are the same yesterday, today, and forever, your faith remains constant and transcends time. Give me faith to sustain my life and saturate my future generations. In Jesus` name I pray. Amen.

ARE WE THERE YET?

2 Timothy 3:1

Day 55

2nd Timothy 3: 1, *New International Version*
- *But mark this: There will be terrible times in the last days.*

We can admit that at least once in our lives on a trip or even a vacation, whether as a child or even as an adult, we`ve either verbally expressed or mentally thought the question: "Are we there yet?" Whether a car ride is 5 minutes long or 5 hours long, that very question seems to be asked — sometimes more than once! We typically ask this question as we grow impatient with the journey as we wait in anticipation of reaching our destination. The Israelites traversed the wilderness for forty years and probably asked Moses repeatedly, "Are we there yet?" Paul traveled from Church to Church to spread the Gospel, dealing with shipwrecks, snake bites, life threats, stoning, and even prison, probably wondering from time to time: "Are we there yet?" Abraham trusted God by packing up his house to travel to a land to which he did not know of and probably questioned God asking, "Am I there yet?" David, after being anointed King of Israel had to flee for his life by hiding, awaiting God's promise, probably thought at one time or another, "Am I there yet?" Jesus traveled from place to place, from seas to mountains, from land to land, probably asking the question to his Father, "Am I there yet?"

In 2 Timothy 3:1-4, Paul is delivering a prophecy of what the world is going to be like in the last days, showing how dangerous things will be. Paul wrote to Timothy, "There will be terrible times in the last days." Other translations of the bible say, difficult times, perilous times, dangerous times, hard times, grievous times, distressing times, violent times and even terrifying times. Paul continues, "People will be lovers of themselves, lovers of money, boastful, proud, abusive, disobedient to their parents, ungrateful, unholy, without love, unforgiving, slanderous, without self-control, brutal, not lovers of the good, treacherous, rash, conceited, lovers of pleasure rather than lovers of God" (2 Timothy 3:2-4, New International Version). I want to reflect on these Scriptures by asking you a series of questions using Paul`s prophecy as a basis. The directions are simple: If you think the answer is yes, add a point—mentally.

1. Do you know of someone who is conceited; who loves themselves and their money so much that they look down on others?
2. Do you know of someone either personally or collectively that mocks God, swears on God, curses God, rejects God, belittles God or even one that does not fear God?
3. Do you know of someone either personally or collectively who is abusive, whether physically or mentally?
4. Do you know of a child or youth either personally or collectively that is disobedient to their parents or those in authority?
5. Do you know of someone either personally or collectively that is ungrateful? You could give them the whole world and they`d be dissatisfied that it is not super-sized?
6. Do you know of someone either personally or collectively who is slanderous, throwing your name under the bus and in the streets with accusations against you that you did not commit?

7. Do you know of someone either personally or collectively with no self-control, just reckless, ratchet, or even rambunctious, not thinking about their speech and/or actions before acting on them?
8. Do you know of someone either personally or collectively that does not love the Lord?
9. Do you know of someone either personally or collectively who is treacherous—who may have betrayed you or someone you may know? That ride-or-die friend who took your trust and friendship for granted and now considers you their enemy, their opp, or even their hater?
10. Do you know of someone either personally or collectively who is unloving and unforgiving, despite being created by a God who is loving and is forgiving unconditionally?
11. Do you know of someone either personally or collectively that loves pleasure or worldly things over their love of, or absent love of God?
12. Do you know of someone either personally or collectively that acts religiously on Sundays, but rejects God and his principles during the week; in other words, someone who puts on a show in front of the pastor and the bishop and the elder and the church folk, but in their absence, shows their true colors of judgment and unrighteousness?

If you answered yes to either of those twelve questions, then we may be living in such a time as this...a time such as Paul prophesied. What is even more troublesome is if you answered yes to **all** twelve questions, we better be getting our house in order for no man knows the day nor the hour, not even the angels in heaven, nor the Son of Man... when the Lord will return. I now present to you the most important question of them all: Are we there yet? Are we living in a time of trouble? A time of terror? A time of danger? A time of peril? A time of grief? A time of violence? A time of distress? Are we living in a time of money-lovers? A time of boastful people? A time of abusive spouses and relationships? A time of disobedient youth? A time of ungrateful saints? A time of unholy politicians? A time of slanderous co-workers? A time of brutal world leaders? A time of out-of-control people? A time of unloving family members? A time of unforgiving friends? A time of unholy pastors? A time of conceited folks? A time of worldly pleasures? I do not intend to offer a message of gloom and doom, but simply to encourage you to think about the question, "Are we there yet?" Are we living in a time prophesied by Paul? Whether you believe the answer to be yes or no, I've got good news for you! Despite the fact that we may be living in a time such as this, does not mean that we are done living. God's not done with you yet, for if you haven't gotten it all together yet, now is the time to get your house in order. The bible tells us to be hopeful, for when our tenure in this life is over, we will ascend to our heavenly home in Paradise. Be encouraged. Stay strong. Despite the fact that we may be *there*, does not mean that we are done.

Questions:
1. Are we *there* yet?
2. Are you *done* yet?

Prayer:
Father: Prepare me for that day. In Jesus` name I pray. Amen.

HELP WANTED?

Titus 3:10

Day 56

Titus 3:10, *New Living Translation*

- *If people are causing divisions among you, give a first and second warning. After that, have nothing more to do with them.*

Several years after the start of the COVID 19 pandemic, the U.S economy is still struggling in terms of unemployment. The COVID 19 pandemic caused the worst jobless crisis and the highest unemployment rate since 1969. It was reported that as soon as April 2020, individuals were filing an average 6 million unemployment claims in a single week, with the next highest record being 695,000 unemployment claims in 1982. Because of the pandemic, the system became overwhelmed which delayed payments for those in need. The Federal government deems "timely" payments if the state issues funds within 21 days of the initial claim for benefits. In March 2020, 97% of payments were timely—today, only 78%. This affected Americans as bills were deferred, rent postponed, credit card debt accumulated, retirement funds raided, and loans were requested. Despite these troubling facts, as COVID 19 became more manageable, job growth in the U.S improved as many new jobs were created to help bolster the economy and to slow inflation. It is commonplace to see at least three "Help Wanted" signs on any given trip when leaving home. Long story short? People need help. Businesses and organizations need help. The economy needs help. America needs help. But, what do you do when you try to help, but help does not want you?

Paul assigned Titus (another companion of Paul) to go to Crete, an island in Greece, to restore order to a group of churches. Crete was infamous for treachery and greed. The men were mercenaries, cities were unsafe, violent, and corrupt. In short, they needed help; so Paul decided to plant churches there. The Cretans had difficulty assimilating their culture with that of Jesus. The Cretans worshiped Zeus, while Christians worshiped God. The Cretans practiced and observed the laws of the Torah, while Paul urged Christians not to because the laws had been fulfilled with Jesus. Titus had one major task: confront the corrupt leaders of each church and replace them with new leaders. Because the corrupt leaders were misled in their teaching and living, immoral living spread to homes as Titus tried to instill generosity, obedience, integrity, self-control, productivity, and morally healthy living to a group of troubled people. Epimenides, a Greek poet, wrote about the Cretan people, "all Cretans are always liars, evil beasts, lazy gluttons." Paul, recognizing the Cretans` inherent nature, gave Titus this disclaimer: "If people are causing divisions among you, give a first and second warning. After that, have nothing more to do with them" (Titus 3:10, New Living Translation).

In other words, Paul was telling Titus although you are sent to help, not everyone wants to be helped. Give them two chances and if they continue to not listen, teach falsely, and cause tension, move on to someone who wants your help.

In the classroom setting, teachers focus so much energy and attention on the troublemakers. Why? These students tend to come to class with no good intention of learning, no good intention of letting others learn, and no good intention of letting the teacher teach uninterrupted so the students *can* learn. Instead of focusing our attention on those who do not want to be there and who do not desire to learn and grow academically, let us shift our focus to those who do. Teachers like to think we are superheroes—we can save *any* child *any* day and get them to want to learn *any* and *everything* possible for the betterment of themselves. This is a myth. Paul teaches us to try to redirect and warn them twice and if they decide not to change, move on. In a greater perspective, we as Christians are the salt of the earth and we are called to proclaim the Gospel and spread God's love and servitude— especially to those who do not yet have a relationship with the Lord so they can be called home to Christ on that day. Clergy and Christians: it is *impossible* to help everybody. It is *impossible* to save everybody. As much as we like to think we possess that ability, we do not. We start to be so hard on ourselves when we don't seem to be making progress in impacting the lives of those whom we know need it, yet they do not want it. If Jesus could not reach and teach all 12 of his disciples, why do we expect perfection in our impact in attempting to help those who need it? Those who need Christ must first want him and not all people do; however as Christians we must not stop the pursuit of saving those whom we can and begin getting over those whom we cannot reach. The Williams Brothers sang it best: "I`m just a nobody trying to tell everybody about somebody who can save anybody." We can tell everybody, but be okay with not being able to help and save everybody. Spiritual help must first be wanted in order to receive it.

Questions:
1. How do you try to help people spiritually?
2. How would you typically respond to helping someone who seemingly does not want to be helped?
3. How will you respond to helping someone who seemingly does not want to be helped?

Prayer:
Father: Help me to help others. Help me to see that not all people can be helped and not all people want to be helped. Although I am your vessel, you made the vessel. I pray for those who do not have a relationship with you to establish one with you before it is too late. In Jesus` name I pray. Amen.

PHILADELPHIA
Philemon 1:15-16
Day 57

Philemon 1: 15-16, *New Living Translation*

- *Perhaps the reason he was separated from you for a little while was that you might have him back forever—no longer as a slave, but better than a slave, as a dear brother. He is very dear to me but even dearer to you, both as a fellow man and as a brother in the Lord.*

Philadelphia, Pennsylvania: The city was named by William Penn, its founder, as he envisioned a city of religious tolerance where no one would be persecuted. Penn was a Quaker, or a pacifist (practicers of peace, refraining from violence), who faced persecution due to his religious practices. Quakers believe in an "inner light" which comes directly from God. While in Pennsylvania, Penn befriended the local Native Americans and learned dialects in order to better communicate with them. Further, Penn acquired Native American lands through business, not slaughter and conquest. The land, later known as Philadelphia, became known as the City of Brotherly love, which is a combination of two Greek words: love (*phileo*) and brother (*adelphos*). Penn chose this name because he hoped to live in peace and harmony with the Native Americans while many others sought to kill the Natives and steal their lands. "Brotherly love" is not defined as the absence of conflict as conflict is inevitable, but it describes a bond that is not expressed through competition, jousting, gibes, or dares (Philadelphia Encyclopedia), but through affection or warm regards for all people. I present to some and introduce to others *the* book of Philadelphia (brotherly love). A text featuring 66 books, over 1,100 chapters, over 4,500 characters, and over 700,000 words: the bible.

The book of Philemon was written during one of Paul's imprisonments and serves as the shortest letter in the New Testament. Philemon was a Roman citizen from Colossae who became a leader of a church started by Epaphras in Colossae. Philemon owned slaves, most notably, one named Onesimus. Onesimus wronged Philemon (unknown reason) and ran away and came to Paul. Paul mentored Onesimus while imprisoned and eventually became a follower and beloved assistant to Paul. Although Paul wanted to keep Onesimus under his study, he realized this posed conflict so he wrote a letter to Philemon asking him to forgive Onesimus and embrace him as a brother and not a slave because all believers are equal partners since we are all equal recipients of God's grace. This request was deemed a tall order as Philemon had every right to punish Onesimus for his actions or put him in prison. This request is unheard-of-kindness and upsets the status quo, so Paul writes to Philemon, "if you consider me your partner, welcome him as you would welcome me. If he has wronged you in any way or owes you anything, charge it to me" (Philemon 1: 17-18, New Living Translation). Just as Jesus committed the ultimate sacrifice of love by dying for our sins (philadelphia), Paul was willing to sacrifice his life to save and set free a slave whom he had only known for a moment: philadelphia.

Paul is teaching us that in the kingdom of God, we are all equals. We all have 1,001 differences, but one thing makes us equal: grace. The same grace of a man who has sinned 10 million times is the same grace of a child who has sinned ten. Grace is not like gas grades (87, 89, 91). We all require the same grade of grace...the same grade of God. Our titles on earth may differ, but our titles in heaven are all the same. Philadelphia does not mean conflict won`t occur, but it is how you proactively and reactively cope with the conflict that expresses philadelphia. The bible teaches, "We love each other because he loved us first. If someone says, "I love God," but hates a fellow believer, that person is a liar; for if we don't love people we can see, how can we love God, whom we cannot see?" (1 John 4: 19-20, New Living Translation). Philadelphia. The bible also teaches, "By this we know love, that he laid down his life for us, and we ought to lay down our lives for the brothers" (1 John 3:16, English Standard Version). Philadelphia. Obedience may be better than sacrifice, but what if being obedient is to sacrifice for our brothers (and sisters) in Christ? "Love one another with brotherly affection" (Romans 12:10, English Standard Version). Philadelphia. You do not have to be a resident of Philadelphia to practice philadelphia. To everyone you encounter, welcome them to philadelphia (lowercase), a character (not city) of brotherly love!

Questions:

1. How do you define philadelphia?
2. How can you express philadelphia daily just as Jesus does?
3. How does Jesus express philadelphia?

Prayer:

Father: I thank you for your philadelphia type love and your fulfilling grace. Help me to step out of my comfort zone to extend philadelphia to all whom I encounter for the glorification of you and your kingdom. This I ask in Jesus` name. Amen.

THE WINNER`S PLAYBOOK

Hebrews 12:1-2

Day 58

Hebrews 12: 1-2, *New Living Translation*

- *Therefore, since we are surrounded by such a huge crowd of witnesses to the life of faith, let us strip off every weight that slows us down, especially the sin that so easily trips us up. And let us run with endurance the race God has set before us. We do this by keeping our eyes on Jesus, the champion who initiates and perfects our faith. Because of the joy awaiting him, he endured the cross, disregarding its shame. Now he is seated in the place of honor beside God's throne.*

On January 2, 2023 during an NFL game between the Buffalo Bills and Cincinnati Bengals, safety Damar Hamlin suffered a cardiac arrest after tackling Cincinnati wide receiver, Tee Higgins. Hamlin got to his feet, but fell quickly back to the ground. A stretcher and ambulance came onto the field as players, coaches, and family huddled around him while America huddled around their television sets at home, praying for his recovery. First responders administered CPR and gave him oxygen as he was loaded into an ambulance and transported to University of Cincinnati Medical Center, remaining there in critical condition. Spending a total of nine days in the hospital under intense care and supervision, Hamlin was released. Prior to his release, news sources tell us that as Hamlin began to communicate three days after the injury, his first question was, "Did we win?" to which Dr. Timothy Pritts responded, "The answer is yes, Damar, you won. You`ve won the game of life." Just as an athlete must have the heart, mind, and strategy to win, so do we as Christians. Hebrews chapter 12 offers us the winner`s playbook.

The book of Hebrews has an anonymous authorship and an anonymous audience, however the author had close ties to the apostles. The audience was a church community facing persecution and imprisonment because of their association to Jesus. The book`s purpose is twofold: to elevate Jesus as superior to all and to challenge readers to remain faithful to Jesus despite persecution. The author opens by reminding readers that Jesus is God`s imprint on nature as he compares Jesus as being superior to specifics such as angels, Moses, priests, and animal sacrifices. In Hebrews 12: 1-2, the author gives us the strategy to win the game of life: the Winner`s Playbook. Jesus is our coach and we are his players. Let's win!

The author compares our Christian journeys to a footrace and the first thing we must do is acknowledge the crowd ("since we are surrounded by such a huge crowd of witnesses to the life of faith"). The author is telling us the first step to winning is to not get distracted by the crowd. We must remain focused on God no matter what plays the enemy plots, no matter what fan distracts us in the audience, no matter what inclement weather may rise in the middle of the game, no matter the shenanigans of the players on the bench, no matter the tactics of the opposing team; we must remain focused, locked-in, and mentally sharp. In our lives, so many people come to deter and distract us and try to get us off on the wrong track, but we must remain faithful to the game and God. Secondly, we must strip off the weight ("strip off every weight that slows us down"). In other words, we have to stay in shape. We have to strip off clothes of habit and sin that are not like God so we can be fit to win. Thirdly, we must expect trips ("sin that so easily trips us up"). There will be hurdles that inevitably get in our way, but we`ve got to learn to overcome those hurdles by any means necessary: knock them down, jump over them, circumvent them. Don`t let the hurdles hinder victory. Fourthly, we must endure ("let us run with endurance"). To have endurance is having the ability to continue and persevere no matter how unpleasant or difficult the situation, experience, or activity may be. Before Damar Hamlin went into cardiac arrest; he was hit hard, but got up. Keep pushing. How can you win if you don't run the entire race? It is impossible. You must endure. Lastly, you must begin with the end in mind (Covey). The bible says *"keeping our eyes on Jesus, the champion..."* (New Living Translation). It is very challenging to win a race if you have no motivation to run. Jesus, our heavenly home, is the end. We must keep our salvation at the forefront of our minds throughout the race so that we have the desire to keep running.

Acknowledge the crowd, but don`t let them distract you. Strip off any unnecessary weight, expect trips and falls, run with endurance, and begin with the end in mind knowing that the end is Jesus. And if you follow the rules of the winner`s playbook, you`ve already won. We know our coach is Jesus Christ and the bible is our playbook and as long as we follow the lead of the coach and play by the rules, we`ve already won. We`ve already received our trophy; we`ve already received our crown; we`ve already had our victory lap; we`ve already received our congratulations, we`ve already received our reward; we`ve already received our accolade; we`ve already received our accomplishment; we`ve already received our promotion; we`ve already received our props; we`ve already received our victory; we`ve already received our prize; we've already won!

Questions:
1. What step in the Winner's Playbook do you do well? How can you maintain this momentum?
2. What step in the Winner's Playbook do you not perform well? How can you improve in this area?

Prayer:
Father: Thank you for the victory. Thank you for your transparency in teaching me how to win. Help me to be reminded that the "race is not given to the swift or the fastest, but to the one who endures until the end." Give me the strength to endure for I`ve already won. In Jesus` name I pray. Amen.

MAN IN THE MIRROR

James 1:23-24

Day 59

James 1: 23-24, *New Living Translation*

- *For if you listen to the word and don't obey, it is like glancing at your face in a mirror. You see yourself, walk away, and forget what you look like.*

Written by Glen Ballard and Siedah Garrett, "Man in the Mirror", is one of Michael Jackson`s beloved hits of all time. As Michael walks the streets in the winter, he "[sees] the kids in the street, with not enough to eat", asking "Who am I to be blind, pretending not to see their needs / Cause they got nowhere to go." He continues, "It's time that I realize / There are some with no home / Not a nickel to loan" asking, "Could it really be me pretending that they`re not alone?" He continues, "Somebody's broken heart and a washed-out dream / They follow the pattern of the wind, ya see / `Cause they got no place to be / That's why I'm starting with me." The chorus reads: "I`m starting with the man in the mirror / I'm asking him to change his ways / And no message could have been any clearer / If you wanna make the world a better place / Take a look at yourself and make a change." The song inspires a message of not only recognizing a problem, but instead of looking to others to fix the problem, we who *can* make a change, must first change ourselves.

James, Jesus` half brother, became a leader in the mother church of Jerusalem as Peter moved from Jerusalem to start new churches. With James as leader, the church experienced hard times with famine and persecution. Through these experiences, the book of James serves to teach and impart wisdom to every and any Jesus community to challenge how one lives, encouraging people to change. James drew influence from Jesus` Sermon on the Mount and Proverbs, the book of wisdom. James begins the letter confirming that life is hard, but life's trials actually serve to produce endurance and shape us into "perfect" individuals. To be "perfect" did not mean to *be* Jesus, but it meant to consistently align one`s actions and speech with that of Jesus, knowing and believing that God is good despite our circumstances. James shares wisdom on favoritism vs. love, genuine faith, the power of the tongue, judging others, truth and honesty, dangers of wealth, having patience, prayer, and uplifting others. In such a short book, James provides wisdom on many topics with one purpose: to change ourselves to be more aligned with Jesus by listening and obeying the Word of God. He writes, "For if you listen to the word and don't obey, it is like glancing at your face in a mirror. You see yourself, walk away, and forget what you look like" (James

1:23-24, New Living Translation). A mirror`s purpose is generally two-fold: to see ourselves *and* to make any necessary changes in our appearance. What, then, becomes the purpose of the mirror if we look at ourselves, see things that need to be changed, yet refrain from changing them? The mirror does not possess the magic to change; we have to start with the man *in* the mirror.

"Man in the Mirror" was rooted in an outward purpose, meaning Jackson saw the world around him and sought to change himself to make a difference. The book of James teaches more of an inward purpose, rooted in changing ourselves first, so that we can make a difference in the world. How? By being selfish. Selfishness is not always negative. We sometimes have to be selfish so that we can be "self-filled." At times we sacrifice our own self-growth or self-care either intentionally or unintentionally to satisfy or please the spouse we live with, or that partner we can't say "no" to, or that job we need to keep the lights on. But how can we measure our true impact as a Christian if we are not truly ourselves, not having the time and space to *be* ourselves and *change* ourselves? When the Devil defeats you at your lowest, really, what has he won? We all need time, space, support, and understanding from others to change ourselves because when it is time for Jesus to return, "each of us will give a personal account to God" (Romans 14:12, New Living Translation). There is no "+1" when entering heaven; it's only one—ourselves. I am not arguing that change happens overnight, but you have to start somewhere. Look at yourself in the mirror, walk away, and remember what you look like so you can change for the better. Start with the man in the mirror.

Questions:

1. When you look in the mirror, what do you see: physically, mentally, socially, emotionally, spiritually?
2. When you look in the mirror, what do you *need* to change? Why?
3. What steps can you take to initiate the change?

Prayer:

Father: Change me; change my heart; change my mind; change my spirit; change my ways; change my habits; change my attitude; change my decisions; change my will; change my ways; change anything that is not like you. Help me to first look at the man in the mirror and not the people around me for change begins with me. In Jesus` name I pray. Amen.

DON`T CUT CORNERS

1 Peter 2:7-8

Day 60

---

1 Peter 2: 7-8, *New Living Translation*

- *"The stone that the builders rejected has now become the cornerstone." And, "He is the stone that makes people stumble, the rock that makes them fall."*

Quoted from the *Oxford Magazine and Church Advocate* (Vol. III, October 1863), "I do not believe, either, in what we used to call cutting corners or going short roads to places. The short road I have always found is in the end the longest. There are more gates to open, more stiles to get over, something or other to hinder, and the distance we save, we lose in the time we take. Set one man to go to a place four miles off by the road; set another to go a short cut across the fields, and ten to one the man on the road gets there first. And it is natural he should, for the road is the legitimate way, the one that has been tried and found the best, and by going straight on it we shall gain time if not distance." The term "cutting corners" is described as undertaking a task in the easiest, quickest, or cheapest way possible by ignoring the rules or omitting steps. Taking a trip into our own hands despite the path of the GPS by creating our own shortcut, skipping steps in instruction manuals we deem "not necessary", heating a meal using the microwave when the directions call for oven usage are all examples of cutting corners. In instances such as these, we find that although we cut corners, the time we take dealing with unforeseen issues that arise in doing so, we could have just done the task the correct way, followed the directions as written, and navigated the route as given. Just as we should not cut corners in our natural lives, we can't cut corners in our spiritual lives either. Don`t cut corners.

Simon was a follower of Jesus and after his confession of Jesus, Jesus renamed him Peter. Peter was called to carry the Good News beyond the borders of Israel. This letter is said to be written by Peter`s co-worker, Silvanus, encouraging churches to endure amidst their suffering as this persecution and hardship paradoxically deepens faith. In 1 Peter 2, Peter reminds us of our status as the chosen people, a royal priesthood, a holy nation, and God's very own possession" (1 Peter 2:9, New Living Translation). Peter calls believers "living stones" that God is using to build his spiritual temple just as Jesus serves as the "Chief Cornerstone." Naturally, a cornerstone is one in which forms a corner that adjoins two walls; remove it, the structure loses support and crumbles and falls. Spiritually, Jesus acts as the cornerstone as it is he who joins people together. Paul writes in Galatians 3:28, "There is no longer Jew or Gentile, slave or free, male and female. For you are all one in Christ Jesus" (New Living Translation). Jesus was a carpenter, yet it is he, the cornerstone, who makes us one and equal in the body of Christ. If we "cut" Jesus or reject him as the builders of the time did, how can we as "temples" be supported"? We can`t, for we`ll crumble and fall under the weight of the Devil. Don't cut corners for Christ.

Matthew 7 teaches us that if we build a house on a firm foundation (symbolic cornerstones), when rain and wind comes, our house won't collapse because of the foundation. If builders cut corners in building a foundation, the building itself becomes futile or purposeless. Have you ever wondered why roads are placed where roads are placed? In other words, why do roads take a certain path? Road engineers don't just lay a road haphazardly, rather it is a systematic and complex task that involves many factors: environmental considerations (wetlands, plants, animals), soil conditions, terrain, property ownership, earthwork, other connecting roads, and residential and business locations. In the opening quote of this devotional from the Oxford Magazine, two men travel a path: one follows a road, while the other makes a shortcut through a field. The reason why the man who takes the longer path down the road will get there first in all cases is because the road is the tried and true way that has been tested, assessed, and proven to be the optimal route. The man who takes the shortcut can`t see the danger of snakes, don`t know where sinkholes or puddles are, and may not run into passersby in case he needs help because the passersby, too, took the road. Live for Christ to your fullest potential as he gives us his 100% daily for "Jesus Christ is the same yesterday, today, and forever" (Hebrews 13:8, New Living Translation). The builders rejected him. You do not have to. Don`t cut corners for Christ.

Questions:

1. How often do you cut corners in life?
2. How often do you cut corners, spiritually or within the confines of your religion?
3. How can you limit cutting corners in the natural and spiritual realms of your life?

Prayer:

Father: Thank you for never cutting corners with me. As I walk with you daily, help me to avail myself to you fully; help me to live for you fully; help me to be for you fully. I cast down any thought of cutting corners I may possess as I live in Christ. In Jesus` name I pray. Amen.

WHO'S YOUR MASTER?

2 Peter 2:19

Day 61

---

2 Peter 2:19, *New Living Translation*

- *They promise freedom, but they themselves are slaves of sin and corruption. For you are a slave to whatever controls you.*

We live under the misconception that slavery ended with the signing of the Emancipation Proclamation by Abraham Lincoln on January 1, 1863. The Emancipation Proclamation didn't instantly free any enslaved people. We live under the misconception that slavery ended officially in 1865 with the ending of the Civil War, noting that on June 19, 1865 a ship led by General Gordon Granger arrived in Galveston, Texas announcing the "freedom" of African Americans, hallmarking Juneteenth. We live under the misconception that slavery ended officially with the signing of the 13th amendment, formally abolishing slavery. Slavery is defined in multiple ways according to the Merriam-Webster Dictionary: "the practice of slaveholding, the state of a person who is held in forced servitude, or submission to a dominating influence." Slavery is not dead; it is very much alive. Slavery is all about control. On slave plantations, slave masters pitted slaves against each other to assert control and raise tension and resentment amongst African Americans. Dark-skinned slaves worked the field while light-skinned slaves worked in the house. Another tactic of control was the notion of buck-breaking, where white slave owners would rape black men in front of other slaves to break their spirit and their masculinity to assert dominance by showing other slaves they had no leader as slaves were raped through forced submission. Other tactics were employed during the time of slavery, showing it is rooted in control. Slavery is not dead; it is very much alive.

2 Peter is addressed to the same audience as 1 Peter. Peter learns he will soon die and this letter serves as his final challenge, seeking to restore confidence and order to church communities. Peter hoped for his letter to be passed down from generation to generation as he attempted to address two major objections and accusations of Jesus` teachings: that Jesus` resurrection was not true and that God's final reckoning or "Judgment Day" was not coming. Peter opens the book, inviting people to be participants of God's life and love by living the seven traits of Jesus: goodness, knowledge, self-control, godliness, endurance, family affection, and love. As Peter is trying to debunk the myth that God`s reckoning was never coming, he attacks the religious leaders and teachers for their wrongful interpretation of freedom. The leaders believed that Jesus` freedom allowed them license to do whatever

they wanted, but Peter reminds the leaders that "[you] promise freedom, but are slaves of sin and corruption..."(2 Peter 2:19, New Living Translation). In other words, freedom for a believer is living a life obedient and in imitation to that of Christ so that one can be free on earth and ultimately, reach freedom in heaven. Peter continues the verse with the biblical definition of slavery, "...for you are a slave to whatever controls you" (2 Peter 2:19, New Living Translation). Based on this scripture, slavery is the result of being controlled by a dominant or superior force. Slavery is not dead; it is very much alive. If slavery is based on control, who is your master?

As humans, we like to think we have control and have things under control although God is the one who orchestrated, is orchestrating, and will orchestrate anything and everything. We allow things to take control of us, succumbing us right back to the slavery that God liberated us from. We are slaves to drugs and alcohol abuse; we are slaves to gossip and drama; we are slaves to social media; we are slaves to toxic people and situations; we are slaves to money or lack thereof; we are slaves to sex; we are slaves to relationships; we are slaves to public perception; we are slaves to our jobs and careers; we are slaves to sin. Instead of being a slave, walk in the freedom that God provides. Don`t let these sins succumb you to slavery. And when it does, repent. Ask God to forgive you and allow you the strength not to commit that sin again. Succumbing to sin makes the Devil your master. Seeking salvation makes Jesus your Master for he is the greatest man in history. "He had no servants, yet they called Him Master. Had no degree, yet they called Him Teacher. Had no medicines, yet they called Him Healer. He had no army, yet kings feared Him. He won no military battles, yet He conquered the world. He did not live in a castle, yet they called Him Lord, He ruled no nations, yet they called Him King. He committed no crime, yet they crucified Him. He was buried in a tomb, yet He lives today" (Lyle C Rollings III, 2008). And because he lives today, we are free. Exercise your freedom by making Jesus your master!

Questions:
1. Who is your Master? In other words, what controls you?
2. What steps can you take to make Jesus your Master—giving more control to him and less control to other aspects or people?

Prayer:
Father: You are my master; I, your masterpiece. Because I am your masterpiece, I submit and surrender every part of me to you. I ask that you break every chain that has me bound to sin and release me to my destiny of freedom. Give me the endurance for the journey. In Jesus` name I pray. Amen.

WHAT`S GOD`S LOVE LANGUAGE?

1 John 4:9-10

Day 62

---

1 John 4: 9-10, *New Living Translation*

- *God showed how much he loved us by sending his one and only Son into the world so that we might have eternal life through him. This is real love—not that we loved God, but that he loved us and sent his Son as a sacrifice to take away our sins.*

In 2006, Amy Winehouse released a single called "Love Is a Losing Game" writing, "For you, I was a flame / Love is a losing game / Five-story fire as you came / Love is a losing game / One I wished I never played / Oh, what a mess we made / And now the final frame / Love is a losing game." Recognizing that love is such a complex emotion, Winehouse argued that *this* love—*her* love—was a losing game. Human love may fail but one death proves love is a winning game. This death occurred on Calvary, giving life to many—the ultimate sacrifice. This death was sent by love, died by love, rose by love, and conquered by love. Love is often reciprocated and although John 3:16 demonstrates God's love for us, how do we express our love for God? In the year 1992 Gary Chapman wrote a book called "The Five Love Languages: How to Express Heartfelt Commitment to Your Mate." The book outlines five ways partners express and experience love (called love languages), which are gift-giving, acts of service, quality time, words of affirmation, and physical touch. Matthew 15:8 writes, "These people honor me with their lips, but their hearts are far from me..."(New Living Translation). "I love you, Lord" rolls off the tongue so easily, but how do we show it? Let's start by identifying God's love language. (Note: God represents both Father and Son).

1 John is not a letter, rather it is deemed a sermon. 1 John`s author is anonymous, while 2 & 3 John are attributed to the "disciple, whom Jesus loved." Much of the wording and teaching of 1 John comes from the Gospel according to John; this John simply wants to remind Christians to stay true to what they already believe. 1 John offers two major metaphors about God: God is Light and God is Love. According to 1 John, "walking in the light" means following Jesus` commands; but even if you fail, Jesus` death atones for sin. Secondly, God is Love, defined as giving up one's life as a sacrifice for others demonstrated through Jesus` resurrection. God loves us so deeply he chose not to exist without us despite our sins; but how do we demonstrate our love for God using Chapman's love languages as a frame?

The first love language is gift-giving. Matthew 2:11 writes, "They entered the house and saw the child with his mother, Mary, and they bowed down and worshiped him. Then they opened their treasure chests and gave him gifts of gold, frankincense, and myrrh" (New Living Translation). How can *you* gift Jesus? The second love language is acts of service, which is the epitome of Jesus` mission and love. Most notably, just before the Passover festival, Jesus washed his disciples' feet (John 13). Other acts of service include teaching the Gospel, feeding 5,000, healing the sick and many others. What acts of service can you conduct to show your love for God? The third love language is quality time. Jesus did not commission the disciples and let them be, he spent quality time with them, leading by example, teaching the Gospel and baptizing people. The fourth love language is words of affirmation, or words that speak life, love, and appreciation for someone. There are several examples within the bible but one that encapsulates them all is when Paul quotes Jesus who said, "My grace is sufficient for you, for my power is made perfect in weakness" (2 Corinthians 12:9, New International Version), reminding us that his grace is everlasting and even when we are at our weakest, he is at his strongest. The last love language is physical touch. There are countless examples of Jesus touching the sick and healing them. Jesus touched a man with leprosy; Jesus touched Peter's mother in law, Jesus touched two blind men; Jesus touched a deaf man; Jesus touched a blind man. Conversely, there are several examples of people who touched Jesus and were healed: the woman with the issue of blood, a man of disease, and various crowds. His touch is a touch of love.

To think that God loves you so much that he saw fit to create a world with you in it is a love that surpasses all loves. He's crazy in love with you. He's head over heels for you. You`re the apple of his eyes. He loves you to the moon and back. He has puppy love for you. He is your lovebird. You take his breath away. He has butterflies-in-the-stomach kind of love for you. He has the hots for you. He is your flame. He is lovey-dovey with you. He's not your better half, he's your best half. He is your one and only. He is your match made in heaven. He is your hubby, your babe, your boo, your baby, your crush, your honey, your bride, your groom. He loved you at first sight and will never stop loving you. He loves you to death. He is your heartbeat. He loves you from the bottom of his heart. He wears your heart on his sleeve. He is your Mr. Right. He is your main squeeze. He is God and like him there is no other. He's shown his love. If you don't know how to love him, begin with the love languages: act in service for him, offer him words of affirmation and praise, reach and stretch your arms to touch him, spend quality time with him and his Word, gift him in love (for self, for others, for him). Speak in a language he understands: love. Live in his love!

Questions:
1. Why do you love God?
2. How do you love God?
3. How can you love God (consider the five love languages)?

Prayer:
Father: Thank you for loving me. Help me to not only say "I love you", but show I love you. Because of your love for me, you sent love to die for me and for that I owe you all of me. Help me to deliver the love you so deserve. In Jesus` name I pray. Amen.

YOU`RE (NOT) WELCOME

2 John 1:10-11

Day 63

---

2 John 1: 10-11, *Amplified Bible*

- *If anyone comes to you and does not bring this teaching [but diminishes or adds to the doctrine of Christ], do not receive or welcome him into your house, and do not give him a greeting or any encouragement.*

With the array of mobile communication available to the world today, it should not be commonplace for guests to impede in your space unannounced. "In-laws" that happen to be "in the neighborhood" want to stop by "just to see and check on you." Grandparents who don`t get out of their houses often happen to be shopping at a store near your home and stop by "just to see their grandbabies." Neighbors who get bored when their spouse is at work or their children are at school knock on the door because they "just need something to do and someone to talk to" until their family returns. Friends who show up to your social gathering or party after not receiving an invitation and you have to muster up the strength to smile and say "I meant to send you an invitation; c`mon in" just to accompany and be considerate of their feelings. Co-workers who take advantage of what was supposed to be a five second conversation of "Hi, how are you?" followed by "good" come to your desk while you are eating or working on a project and unload their entire day and lives on you as you have to pretend like you are listening and necessarily care. It happens to all of us. The world's most genuine and faithful extrovert doesn't possess the desire to entertain people 24/7 showing that sometimes you`re not welcome.

To reiterate, 1, 2, and 3 John addresses communities who broke off from churches, no longer acknowledging Jesus as the Messiah. This act caused hostility to those who remained faithful. 2 John is issuing a warning to a specific house church warning them that deceivers (people who deny Jesus) are on the way seeking validation for their wrongful teaching. John is writing to this church asking them not to offer the deceivers any encouragement for their false doctrine. John writes, "If anyone comes to you and does not bring this teaching [but diminishes or adds to the doctrine of Christ], do not receive or welcome him into your house, and do not give him a greeting or any encouragement" (2 John 1:10-11, Amplified Bible). In other words, John is stating not to welcome non-believers into your circle, nor should you encourage them in their evil ways. To "greet" these deceivers is to show them hospitality and John is stating not to welcome them publicly into the church for them to promote false teaching, hindering the work and momentum they already had established in the faithful communities of Jesus.

We as Christians are defined by what we reject as much as by what we accept. You teach what you tolerate whether directly or indirectly. If you teach godliness and accept evil, you are promoting it—though it may be indirectly. Countless times I have been in situations where people have invaded my house (symbolic of my space) with evil thoughts and actions and countless times instead of taking the higher road I laugh and smile in their faces, seemingly condoning their actions. John tells us not to encourage such behavior. By seemingly encouraging wrongful behavior (whether directly or indirectly), all we are doing is exacerbating the issue at hand and not correcting the behavior. The bible says "For the Lord disciplines those he loves, and he punishes each one he accepts as his child" (Hebrews 12:6, New Living Translation). Just as Jesus corrects those whom he loves and those who belong to him, we as Christians are supposed to do the same to those we encounter who are not acting in accordance with God's love and law. Simply put, if someone comes to your house or your event uninvited and unwelcome and you keep allowing them to do so without expressing to them you don't want them there, they will continue to show up uninvited and unwelcome, thinking their presence is accepted and appreciated. And if you allow it, you never correct the issue. The same applies to life. Don`t greet (show hospitality) and welcome into your home or space those who oppose God's love and law; for when you do, you condone the behavior and feed into the devil's trap. John did not say oppose those who do not know God or those seeking to know him, but oppose those who are deliberately acting in a means that is not of God. Tell those people "you're not welcome."

Questions:
1. How can you handle those who you do not welcome (those who actively oppose God and his law)?
2. How can you discipline yourself (though you seek godliness) when you fail to act in accordance with God's love and law?
3. How can you discipline those whom you love (those who seek godliness) when they fail to act in accordance with God's love and law?

Prayer:
Father: Give me the discernment to welcome those that are of you and give me the strength, discipline, and ability to not welcome those who oppose you. Allow me not to tolerate what you do not teach and allow me not to condone things that are not of your character. This I ask in Jesus` name. Amen.

FACE TO FACE

3 John 1:13-14

Day 64

---

3 John 1:13-14, *New Living Translation*

- *I have much more to say to you, but I don't want to write it with pen and ink. For I hope to see you soon, and then we will talk face to face.*

Good news. Bad news. They both have their places in our lives and they both have different approaches for delivery. What I find so interesting is that no matter how bad the news or how good the news, it is customary that we share it in person, face to face. A girlfriend wants to break up with her boyfriend; how does she do it? Face to face. A manager is prepared to terminate you; how does he or she do it? *After* you've worked your entire shift, but face to face. A spouse wants to share the news of receiving a promotion on the job; how do they share it? With the family, face to face. A bill collector or bank personnel has tried to reach you multiple times to no avail; how do they get you to respond? A representative visits you face to face on your job or at your home. A birthday or anniversary, news of pregnancy, a college acceptance—all news one wishes to share face to face. On the contrary, the death of a family member, news someone has been in a severe accident, or even a life-traumatizing event—all news one does not want to share face to face, yet it is best to do so given the severity of the situation and the ability to act as support for the recipient of the news. As COVID-19 impacted the world as we know it, many school districts went to hybrid or virtual learning. Teachers taught and students learned remotely from home using a variety of communication or peer-to-peer software such as ZOOM, Google Meet, or Microsoft Teams. As COVID-19 became more manageable, teachers all over the world grew optimistic as students were welcomed back into the classroom for face-to-face learning to try to recoup the learning loss occurring on virtual platforms for almost a year and a half. When you think about this idea of news sharing, the best or the worst news is usually told face to face, not through text, letter, or email. Are you ready to receive your news face to face?

3 John is written to one of the house church members named Gaius. John is asking Gaius to welcome legitimate missionaries who will arrive soon because the leader of the church (Diotrephes) is rejecting anyone associated with John the Elder. Although John is writing this letter, he writes something unique in it that acts as the message of this devotional. John writes, "When I come, I will report some of the things he is doing and the evil accusations he is making against us. Not only does he refuse to welcome the traveling teachers, he also tells others not to help them. And when they do help, he puts them out of the church" (3 John 1:10, New Living Translation). The keywords here are "When I come." John ends the letter, "I have much more to say to you, but I don't want to write them with pen and ink. For I hope to see you soon, and we will talk face to face" (3 John 1:13-14, New Living Translation).

How many of you know that when you put something in writing, it makes it official and legitimate. Speaking transparently, we need to watch *who* and *how* we gossip about people. John, in this letter, expresses animosity and opposition about Diotrephes, but he ensures that he does not gossip in his letter. All John tells us is the facts of the matter: Diotrephes is a haughty control freak that is making evil accusations, refusing the travelers of Christ, and telling others not to assist them; and if they do, they are put out of the church. As much as John wants to belittle, insult, curse at, curse out, or speak ill of Diotrephes in this letter, he saves this for a meeting with the people of the church face to face. Why? Because John knows "all you have in this world is your word." I am not encouraging you to confront your conflicts face to face, but rather watch what you write. That email you send to your co-workers about your supervisor; that new group text you create to talk trash about one friend in the main group chat, that note that you write to one church member about another church member, that social media post you try to hide from the person you`re talking about can *all* be traced back to you somehow and that is one fight you do not want to be caught in. If you speak to someone face to face, unless they record you, there is no proof of what you said. But the second you put something in writing, it can and will be held against you. Watch what you write and to whom you write it too. Use your writing for good and not evil as the bible says, "Write the vision and make it plain" (Habakkuk 2:2, King James Version). A law isn't a law until it is written. Scripture wasn't Scripture until it was written. The commandments weren't the commandments until they were written. You`re not a citizen of heaven until your name is first written. The bible says in Revelation 20:15, "Anyone whose name was not found *written* in the book of life was thrown into the lake of fire" (Revelation 20:15, New International Version). Watch what you write.

At the beginning of this devotional, I asked you the question, "Are you ready to receive your news face to face?" You may be wondering what news I am writing about. I am referring to your acceptance letter into heaven. Jesus does not send you a text message, an email, a tweet, a post, a snap, a Tik Tok, a DM, a letter, or a report concerning your good news. Revelation 22:4 writes, "And they will see his face" (New Living Translation) and he will tell us face to face, "Well done, my good and faithful servant" (Matthew 25:21).

Questions:

1. Are you ready to receive your good news from God face to face?
2. How can you assure you receive your good news from God?

Prayer:

Father: I can only imagine meeting you face to face. There is so much beauty in the world that leaves us in awe, I wait in great anticipation to see you face to face. Teach me, guide me, lead me to your presence so that I can receive my good news from you, face to face. In Jesus` name I pray. Amen.

LOVED AND FEARED

Jude 1:22-23

Day 65

Jude 1: 22-23, *New King James Version*

- *And on some have compassion, making a distinction; but others save with fear, pulling them out of the fire, hating even the garment defiled by the flesh.*

In the year 1513, Niccolo Machiavelli wrote a political treatise called "The Prince." The premise of the text gave direction on how to be an effective ruler. One of the questions Machiavelli raises is: is it better to be loved or feared? As he answers the question, he recalls previous rulers, ranking them on levels of cruelty to compassion. Conclusively, Machiavelli answers, "one would prefer to be both [loved and feared] but, since they don't go together easily, if you have to choose, it's much safer to be feared than loved." Machiavelli continues, "Love binds when someone recognizes he should be grateful to you, but, since men are a sad lot, gratitude is forgotten the moment it's inconvenient. Fear means fear of punishment, and that's something people never forget. A ruler can't expect to inspire love when making himself feared." The issue is either black or white; there is no gray—no in-between, according to Machiavelli. Machiavelli concludes that although he rather be feared than loved, "people decide for themselves whether to love [their ruler]…it's the ruler who decides whether they're [the people] going to fear him" and because of this, what a sensible ruler must do is not focus on whether he is loved or feared, but "take care that people don't hate him." Is God feared or loved?

Jude (or "Judah") was one of Jesus` four brothers, who became Jesus` disciple after Jesus` death. All four of the brothers became leaders in Jewish Christian communities. Jude was a traveling teacher and missionary as he challenged Christians to contend for the Christian faith because corrupt teachers were spreading. He urges Christians to stay away from these teachers, showing evidence that rebellious people always receive God's justice (Israelites, Sodom and Gomorrah) and rebellious people can corrupt others (Cain, Balaam the Sorcerer, and Korah the Levite). Jude uses several metaphors to demonstrate the meaningless nature of the corrupt teachers, comparing them to selfish shepherds who care only for themselves, clouds with no rain, chaotic waves churning up foam for no good deed, dead autumn trees with no fruit, and wandering stars (no good for guidance). Jude now leaves us asking the question: so what do we do to stop these corrupt teachers? Jude declares, "And on some have compassion, making a distinction; but others save with fear, pulling them out of the fire, hating even the garment defiled by the flesh" (Jude 1: 22-23, New King James Version).

An English proverb writes, "Different strokes for different folks", meaning different things appeal to different people. Similarly, wisdom, learning, and understanding are not a one-size-fits-all concept. In other words, Jude is saying in this Scripture that we as Christians must make the distinction about these corrupt teachers. On some, have compassion by teaching them what is right and just through acts of love. No matter how misleading the person is, it is our duty to love them and be compassionate concerning their salvation. Others—you have to scare with fear in a more strong and assertive manner. In fear, however, don't become prideful as if you're exempt from judgment and hell. Instead, incite fear through the lens of God. Children are taught similarly. You may have one child who you can ask kindly not to do something and they comply; whereas you may have another you have to give them "that look" or threaten them a few times to get them to comply. Whatever the case may be, we as Christians must teach and proclaim the Gospel through love and fear for we serve a God who is both. The bible says in Psalms 2:11, "Serve the Lord with reverent (respect) fear" (New Living Translation), recognizing he has ultimate power to serve justice as he pleases; secondly "continue to love one another, for love comes from God" (1 John 4:7, New Living Translation). Machiavelli argued a ruler can`t be feared *and* loved, however God is the proof that having both love and fear can make you the greatest ruler to ever live. He is both.

Questions:

1. How does God inspire fear?
2. How does God inspire love?
3. Is God more loving or fearful? Why?

Prayer:

Father: I thank you for your Word. I realize that everyone who cries "Lord, Lord" is not of you. Give me the wisdom, knowledge, and understanding to teach and obey your Word, serving you with both love and reverent fear. This I ask in Jesus` name. Amen.

KNOCK, KNOCK: WHO'S THERE?

Revelation 1:18 ; Revelation 3:7 ; Revelation 3:20

Day 66

Revelation 1:18, *New Living Translation*

- *I am the living one. I died, but look—I am alive forever and ever! And I hold the keys of death and the grave.*

Revelation 3:7, *New Living Translation*

- *"Write this letter to the angel of the church in Philadelphia. This is the message from the one who is holy and true, the one who has the key of David. What he opens, no one can close; and what he closes, no one can open:*

Revelation 3:20, *New Living Translation*

- *"Look! I stand at the door and knock. If you hear my voice and open the door, I will come in, and we will share a meal together as friends.*

In Shakespeare's play, *Macbeth,* we encounter a porter, who is the gate-keeper to King Macbeth. Upon hearing someone knock at the gate, he says "That`s a lot of knocking. If a man were the porter of the gate to Hell, he'd have a lot of key-turning to do." The porter, jokingly, personifies the gate-keeper to Hell asking, "Knock, knock: Who's there? A farmer who hung himself after hoarding goods, hoping to charge high prices during a famine that never came." He continues, "Knock, knock: Who's there? A smooth-talker who would swear under oath to both sides of an argument, committing treason for God's sake for he could not even smooth-talk his way into heaven." He proceeds, "Knock, knock: Who's there? An English tailor who skimped on fabric for fancy clothes; come on in [to Hell], tailor; it's hot enough to hear your iron in here." The porter ends his fantasy impersonation saying, "Knock, knock: Who's there? But this place is too cold for Hell. I won't be the devil`s porter any longer. I think I would have let in someone from every profession that takes the high road to Hell." Though this impersonation has a humorous effect and purpose, it portrays a true message of reality: the door to hell is a revolving one and Jesus holds the key to it. Will you knock at the door of doom (Hell) or the door of deliverance (Heaven)? The choice is yours.

The book of Revelation is a book rich in symbolism and imagery. It is not a code to crack when Jesus will return, but serves as a revelation (dream or vision) that reveals the final outcome of the world, acting as a warning to people. The letters were written by John (beloved disciple or a Messianic prophet) and sent to seven churches. John was exiled to the island of Patmos and saw a vision of Jesus exalted as Jesus addresses problems in the churches. In Revelation 1, Jesus establishes his authority, writing, "I am alive forever and ever! And I hold the keys of death and the grave" (Revelation 1:18, New Living Translation). Jesus never lets the Devil borrow the keys for it is Jesus who determines our ultimate destiny. Jesus is the keyholder of life. Later in the book in Revelation 3, John begins his letters to four of the seven churches: Ephesus, Smyrna, Pergamum, and Thyatira. In Revelation 3, Jesus asserts, again, his power, dominion, and authority over our destiny (keys and doors, using the expression "the one who has the key of David" (New Living Translation) to show he determines who is admitted and excluded to each final destination. However, in the 20th verse, Jesus demonstrates that although he holds the keys, we have a choice for the door to which we enter. Jesus declares, "Look! I stand at the door and knock. If you hear my voice and open the door, I will come in, and we will share a meal together as friends" (Revelation 3:20, New Living Translation). Jesus extends the opportunity to both saint and sinner, to share in his love in a meaningful, intimate manner.

Jesus stands at the door of our heart and knocks, waiting for us to let him in. What is so interesting is that Revelation teaches us that Jesus has a key to our heart, to heaven, and to hell, yet it is up to us to let him in. He has a key, but gives us the choice. Notice we do not have to go to his door; he comes to us with the promise that he will come in if we want him to. USPS, UPS, and FedEx drop packages and leave, but Jesus waits, knocking, waiting for him to be received. He won't ring the bell and then bail. He won't knock and leave. The invitation is open to anyone and everyone. John writes that upon the time for Jesus to return, "Let us be glad and rejoice..." (Revelation 19:7, New Living Translation). This union must be one of joy. Put your joy in Jesus and not in the realities of the world for the Devil can easily take the world, but he has no power to overcome it—only Jesus can. Put your joy in him and this day of great expectation. Knock, knock: Who's there? Jesus. Will you let him in? The choice is yours.

Questions:
1. Who visits the door to your heart most often: God or Satan?
2. How can you limit Satan's visitations to your heart and give God full custody?
3. Why, ultimately, do you want Jesus to be in your heart? What are the benefits?

Prayer:
Father: I realize the choice to salvation is mine. Help me to live and lead a life with you not at the door, but with full residence to my heart. Remove any aspect that is not like you and fill me with your light and your love. You are welcome. Come on in. Although Revelation is the last book of the bible, it is not the end for me. I declare and decree that by me choosing to let you in my heart today, that I receive your knocks to bigger, to better, to higher, and to greater as I live in sync with you. In Jesus' name I pray. Amen.

NOTES

NOTES

NOTES

NOTES